Vampires

A Field Guide to the Creatures That Stalk the Night

By

Dr. Bob Curran

Illustrated by Ian Daniels

New Page BOOKS

Franklin Lakes, NJ

VAMPIRES
EDITED AND TYPESET BY KRISTEN PARKES
Cover design by Lu Rossman/Digi Dog Design
Cover and Interior Illustrations by Ian Daniels
Printed in the U.S.A. by Book-mart Press

To order this title, please call toll-free 1-800-CAREER-1 (NJ and Canada: 201-848-0310) to order using VISA or MasterCard, or for further information on books from Career Press.

The Career Press, Inc., 3 Tice Road, PO Box 687,
Franklin Lakes, NJ 07417
www.careerpress.com
www.newpagebooks.com

Library of Congress Cataloging-in-Publication Data

Curran, Bob.
    Vampires: a field guide to the creatures that stalk the night / Bob Curran.
        p.cm.
    Includes index.
    ISBN 1-56414-807-6 (pbk.)
        1. Vampires. I. Title.

    BF1556.c87 2005
    398'.45—dc22

                                                                2005048431

Contents

Introduction

ANCIENT FEARS

ampire. The very word conjures up visions of ruined castles in Eastern Europe; of deathly pale and saturnine noblemen, wrapped in dark cloaks; of fangs brushing the throat of some helpless female; of stakes and crucifixes destroying ancient evil. Such things have become the stock of vampire novels, films, and television programs. And, of course, they bear only the vaguest resemblance to the actual truth, for the vampire is a more complex creature than Hollywood would have us believe.

The idea of the vampire is tied up in ancient notions of death. Like ourselves, peoples across time often wondered what lay on the other side of death but, unlike today, they usually had no context in which to place the Afterlife. Only a few cultures had the concept of reward and punishment after death—a feature of structured religious belief. All they knew was that the dead simply *went somewhere.* This, of course,

prompted other questions: Where did they go? Were they aware of what went on in the world that they'd left behind? Could they intervene in the affairs of those who came after them? What was their relationship with the living? What was the afterlife like? Opinions varied widely.

For the ancient Hebrews, for example, the departed made the journey to Sheol (literally meaning "the grave"), a dank, subterranean place, filled with rivers, lakes, and eternal mist. Here the spirits of the dead wandered aimlessly, barely aware of what was occurring in the world they had left, and they took little interest in the affairs of their descendants. The ancient Egyptians thought that the next world was very much like this one, and that power and status would continue there as it had in the world of the living. Thus, servants were murdered as soon as their masters died so they could continue to serve them beyond their demise. Those who crossed from one plane of existence to the other took nothing with them that had to do with the world that they'd left behind—it was doubtful that they even remembered that world. The Vikings believed that the Afterlife was a great hall known as Valhalla (the Hall of Heroes) that allegedly stretched into infinity to accommodate all the souls that were there. It could only be entered by those Vikings who died in battle or with a sword in their hand. Throughout eternity there were feats of strength, mock battles, drinking, and carousing amongst the dead who assembled there, making it a warrior's paradise. What became of those departed Vikings who died in bed or without a sword is unclear. Those who resided in Valhalla were, of course, much too busy with their revelry and battles to take any account of what happened in the world of the living.

The ancient Celts, on the other hand, believed in a place called the Otherworld, which was a place of the dead and a place of fairies and other supernatural creatures. This unspecified realm has never been properly described and has varied in its description from a beautiful landscape, which inspired bards and poets; to a bleak and dismal place; to an unending

emptiness. From here, the dead could watch the affairs of the world, in which they took a definite interest. Indeed, Celtic tradition taught (as did some other ancient belief systems) that they might from time to time *return* to the living world in order to intervene in the affairs of day-to-day existence. It was not, however, a nebulous, ethereal spirit that returned from the Otherworld, but a solid corporeal entity, which might be pretty much as he or she had been when alive. They might return for a variety of reasons. Sometimes, the dead returned simply to enjoy the life that they had left behind—food, warmth, comfort, the companionship of their loved ones. The dead, it was thought, had the same needs and desires as the living. They might also return for other purposes: to warn, to admonish, to advise, to complete unfinished business, or, occasionally, to take revenge.

But *when* might they return? Although theoretically they might return at any time—and some of them, it was believed, actually did—the common consensus was that they only did so at certain times: when the stars were propitious. In Celtic Western Europe, for instance, the dead mainly returned on two nights of the year: at the festivals of May Eve and Samhain (October 31). These were dates on which the seasons changed. Spring gave way to summer, and autumn yielded to the darkness of winter. Although people now tend to celebrate Halloween (October 31) as the premier supernatural festival, we must also keep in mind that April 30, once widely known throughout the Germanic and Scandinavian worlds as *Walpugisnacht*, was also a time when dark creatures held sway over the world. At such times, the Veil between the worlds of the living and the dead was very thin. The hours of midday and midnight were also transitional periods when the supernatural barriers became almost nonexistent and allowed the dead to cross. We are all familiar with the ghost at midnight (when one day merged into another), but midday (when the morning passed into the afternoon) was also a significant time. Both the ancient Greeks and Romans believed it was when the

legions of the dead, together with the forces of evil, were at their most powerful.

One of the most potent reasons for the dead returning from the grave was to remind those who were living that the dead could still see them and might still watch over them. In some instances, the dead took on the role of moral arbiter, perhaps instructing a descendant to mend his or her ways or to act in a more kindly way toward his or her peers. The tale of Scrooge in Charles Dickens's *A Christmas Carol* contains elements of that ancient belief.

Christian Dogma and Vampires

The spread of structured and organized religion—Christianity, in particular—brought about a profound change in how the living viewed the returning dead. For instance, in Celtic Western Europe, the Christian Church had to contend with old, pagan beliefs, many of which it incorporated, in modified forms, into the Church's own religious dogma. One such belief was the notion of the Celtic Otherworld to which spirits went after death. This, of course, did not completely fit in with the Church's structured notions of heaven and hell, where rewards and punishments were meted out. So, it seems, a form of compromise was reached. Like many other pagan ideals, the otherworld became incorporated into the Christian canon in the guise of purgatory, a place of waiting and testing for the soul before it achieved its final reward or punishment. This was a clever compromise, because it not only successfully incorporated ancient beliefs, it also had the potential to make money for the Church. The soul could be released from purgatory, it was believed, only through having prayers and Masses formally said for it. And the only person who could do this was the priest, who had to be paid for doing so. Consequently, a special day was set aside for the remembrance of the dead when Masses were said for the repose of their souls: All Saint's Day

(November 1). This coincided with the ancient Celtic festival of Samhain, a day for remembering the dead. The Church now taught that God permitted the departed to return on the evening before All Souls Day to remind the living of their obligation to them. If their families were neglectful of such obligations, the dogma continued, and the angry dead might take physical revenge against them. Moreover, the dead who had not been correctly buried according to the rites of the Church (when, once again, the priest had to be paid) might be permitted to return to punish those who survived them for their miserliness and neglect.

The notion of the angry and vengeful dead quickly caught on; it was Church dogma, after all. It was thought that the returning dead—substantial and near corporeal entities—might attack the property of their remaining family, such as their cattle and other livestock. From the necks of the animals they might drink blood, causing the creature to be weak and useless. And sometimes, in an act of ultimate revenge, the material cadaver might even attack the family and drink *their* blood. The myth of the vengeful, blood-drinking dead was being created.

But it was not only the Christian religion that was the basis of the vampire motif. Other religious structures had their own orthodoxies and to disobey these was to invite supernatural retaliation. There were other elements as well—religious and national differences; differing ethnic and cultural perspectives; the personality of the person concerned—all of which could create a vampire. The foreigner, the scold, the misanthrope, the person with a different religious or cultural viewpoint all could become a dangerous revenant after their demise. Not only might they attack their own families but they might savage other members of the community as well. Gradually, a whole mythos was created around the dead—a mythos of which there were many versions, depending on the religion and culture involved.

Almost every culture (past and present) in the world has its beliefs regarding the returning dead, and all of these reflected

the perspectives of the culture that produced it. Therefore, no generalization about the vampire can be given, for there are as many vampires as there are stories about them. Much of our so-called "knowledge" about vampires derives, arguably, from two sources: the novel *Dracula* (written by an Irishman, Bram Stoker, from a Christian perspective) and Hollywood (which has largely formed its images from Stoker's novel). For instance, we believe that the crucifix (a distinctly Christian symbol) will repel the vampire, but what if the vampire is Jewish? We understand that a stake driven through the heart will destroy the vampire but, depending on the locality, the type of wood used is crucial. Not to mention, a stake driven through the heart will only temporarily *suspend* the vampire, not destroy it. We are almost conditioned to believe that vampires come from Transylvania in Eastern Europe and have the power to turn themselves into blood-drinking bats. Whilst there *are* tales of the Undead in Eastern Europe, they are not called vampires. And, of course, the blood-drinking vampire bat is native to *South America.* (The word *vampire* is thought to be of ancient Turkish origin and is entomologically related to the word *oupir* from Southern Russia. It is now thought to be obsolete in Turkish.)

We are all familiar with the vampire taking its sustenance from the neck of some paralyzed individual (usually some voluptuous sleeping girl). This looks good on the celluloid screen, and "the vampire's kiss" contains the necessary eroticism to fill the pages of a book but, once again, it cannot necessarily be generalized. In very few cases the creature drinks from the neck veins (this would, it is argued, instantly kill its victim). Instead, it often drinks from the arms, legs, or other parts of the body. And it is not only blood that is taken. In some cultures vampires do not drink blood at all but rather vital fluids (semen, vaginal issue) usually from young men or women. This, of course, serves to explain the nocturnal emissions, which are still believed to weaken young warriors in some parts of the world.

The notion of the vampire *biting* the neck of its victim is also largely a Hollywood creation based on Stoker's perceptions. Several vampiric creatures, such as the Aswang of the Philippines, uses a hollow tongue through which it draws bodily fluids, whilst a Vietnamese vampire uses certain antennae that protrude from its nose in order to ingest blood and semen. Nor, as we shall see, is the vampire necessarily a *nocturnal* creature, though many of them are; it can appear at any time, including midday.

The dead, it seems, are everywhere, and they can physically attack the living. The dead *hate* the living, it is thought, with a passion no one can truly understand, and the vampire is the embodiment of that hatred.

Today, of course, the vampire has become something of a stereotype (mainly due to Stoker's novel, in which the Undead became something of a metaphor for a number of other issues that permeated 19th-century English life—the role of women, relations with the aristocracy, and so on) through both mass-market literature and cinema. We now equate the vampire with the likes of Bela Lugosi and Christopher Lee, or with such popular television programs as *Buffy the Vampire Slayer* and *Angel*, which have now been translated into a number of languages and aired in many countries around the world. None of these bear much resemblance to original vampire beliefs, but the enduring interest and their mass appeal **does** serve to show that, even in the modern-day world, our unease at the possible imminence of the dead has not quite gone away. The vampire still lies at the heart of the human psyche.

This book seeks to celebrate the vampire in its widest possible context: its diversity and cultural distinctiveness all across the world. Forget the "thing in the cape"; here are vampires perhaps you didn't know about, lurking everywhere, deep in the shadows of every corner of the planet. No matter where you are, whether late at night or in the middle of the day, the restless, malignant dead may be closer than you think!

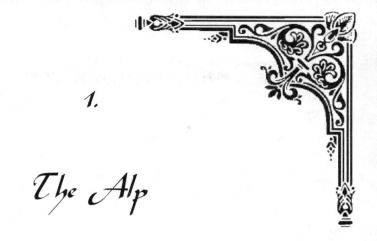

1.

The Alp

GERMANY/AUSTRIA

Although now heavily industrialized, Germany was once a land of mystery, swathed in thick forests and boasting bleak mountains and remote lakes. The folklore of the country reflected a sense of eeriness and awe. Indeed, many of our best-known fairytales come from this part of the world—*Sleeping Beauty*, *Little Red Riding Hood*, and *Rumplestiltskin*—and are allegedly dark old peasant tales that were adapted and sanitized by English Victorians. Originally, it is believed, many of these tales were practically horror stories—filled with werewolves, child-stealing goblins, and cannibal witches, all of whom were believed to dwell in the forest depths of mountain fastness. Here, too, were the hostile spirits that characterized the sullen landscape and who viewed

mankind with mistrust and belligerence. These were the forces that shaped the brooding trends in early Germanic folklore.

Cannibalism and blood drinking appear in some of the stories from the German forests. The flesh-eating witch in the story of *Hansel and Gretel* and the malignant goblin in *Rumpelstiltskin* (where there are overtones of carrying away and devouring babies) are typical examples. The woodland depths were alive with all kinds of foul creatures who could threaten humankind.

The Wood Wives

Prevalent amongst these were the *Wood Wives*, who usually kept to the deeper parts of the forest but sometimes ventured close to houses, drawn by smells of cooking or the sounds of human laughter and conversation. They were invariably female, but not necessarily ghosts of the dead, rather elemental forces from the forests. The Wood Wives were ambivalent creatures—tall, elegant, and dressed in green, flowing robes but with deathly pale skin and terrible, rending claws. They could be benevolent, attending to those who had become lost or injured in the forest, but more likely as not, they could kill wandering travellers in order to drink their blood. Huntsmen and woodcutters were especially at risk from them for two reasons: first, they tended to venture deep into the woods and forests, and second, they interfered with the natural balance of nature by hunting animals or cutting down trees. Tales of hunters found dead with their throats torn out and drained of blood found beside woodland trails proliferated through the Germanic countryside in the 16th and 17th centuries. Skeptics might say that such deaths were due to the preponderance of wolves and wild creatures, which were said to dwell in the leafy depths, but for the medieval/early modern mind there could only be one explanation, and that was a supernatural one: the Wood Wives.

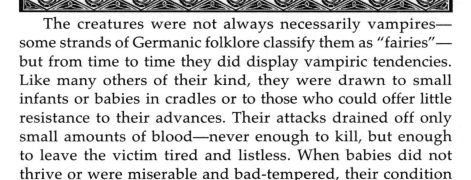

The creatures were not always necessarily vampires—some strands of Germanic folklore classify them as "fairies"—but from time to time they did display vampiric tendencies. Like many others of their kind, they were drawn to small infants or babies in cradles or to those who could offer little resistance to their advances. Their attacks drained off only small amounts of blood—never enough to kill, but enough to leave the victim tired and listless. When babies did not thrive or were miserable and bad-tempered, their condition was blamed on the Wood Wives. When riding through the forests, huntsmen saw the Wood Wives move away amongst the shadows of the trees, but all were scared to approach them.

Because the Wood Wives were bound to nature and with the forest, one of the ways to dispel them was to burn bits of wood in a fire. It was said, particularly in places such as Bavaria, that if this was done, one of the Wood Wives would die, hidden away in the forest glades. However, such measures were risky, for the action might inflame the Wood Wives' anger and cause them to attack.

The Tomtin

Other beings also dwelt in the forest depths. Many of these were believed to be "little people" who went under the general classifications of goblins, elves, dwarves, or trolls. The most vicious of these were the *tomtin*, little men dressed in red (the color of blood) who were known to attack travellers on lonely forest roads. Sadistic creatures, the tomtin were associated, in Germanic folklore, with a number of ancient beings who were said to live even deeper in the forest, venturing out into the world of men only at certain times of the year. These entities were probably the embodiment of old, nearly forgotten forest or fertility gods that had been worshipped by the early German tribes and bore names such as Nacht

Ruprecht (a bizarre and alarming figure, adorned in straw and antlers) and Schwartz Peeter (a grim, black, muscular figure, like a giant blacksmith). The tomtin were considered to be their servants, murdering travellers at their behest. Pulling travellers to the ground, the tomtin beat them with chains or with barbed sticks or poles until they were dead and then commenced to lap at their blood like dogs. They bore back the hearts and livers of those whom they killed as sustenance to their ancient masters amongst the trees.

Many of these entities chose to manifest themselves during the winter months. Nacht Ruprecht, for example, would come to the windows of the cottages and peer in, generally terrifying those within. Accompanied by his close servant, George Oaf, who was armed with a great whip or flail, and with the tomtin thronging after him, he travelled the snow-covered roads, beating and often killing those whom he met. To those who worshipped him, or kept old faiths alive, he offered rewards.

The veneration of these ancient deities alarmed the Church so much that they decided to supplant the idea of a supernatural pagan being travelling around dispensing gifts and rewards with a Christian counterpart. And the person whom the Church chose was St. Nicholas. Ironically, the bloodthirsty, blood-drinking tomtin were now attached to this Christian saint. They did not, however, initially lose any of their brutish and depraved ways. In parts of Germany, St. Nicholas was known as "Buller Claus" (Belled Nicholas) because of the chains and bells that he carried. When he approached a house, the tomtin went ahead to rouse sleeping children, drag them from their beds, and ask them questions on the Christian catechism. If they could not answer or answered incorrectly, the tomtin beat them with sharp sticks whilst St. Nicholas pelted them with hard coal until they bled and the tomtin licked the blood from their wounds. If they were able to answer correctly, they were (grudgingly) rewarded with an apple or sweetmeat.

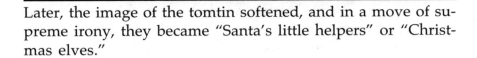

Later, the image of the tomtin softened, and in a move of supreme irony, they became "Santa's little helpers" or "Christmas elves."

The Alp

The idea of cannibalistic, blood-drinking little men, however, continued to permeate both German and Austrian folklore. Ghoulish dwarves, the precursors to Rumpelstiltskin, were said to live in the remote mountains and continued to attack travellers on lonely trails. Gradually, such stories became intermingled with other tales and beliefs—stories of the dead and of werewolves, for example. The notion of returning dead had always been prevalent in Germanic folklore. The dead were hostile toward the living, and they might attack and devour their victims if they so chose—the classic motif for the vampire or werewolf. In some instances, it was believed that the dead tore at their own funeral shrouds and dug into other graves to attack other bodies, which they then devoured. This alleged desecration was of great concern to early-modern churchmen. In 1679, the German theologian Phillip Rohr published a treatise titled *De Masticatione Mortnorum (On the Chewing Dead)*, which was a seminal contribution of vampire literature. In it, the learned churchman discussed beliefs concerning the dead who returned from the tomb to bite and chew (manduction) from a religious viewpoint. The text demonstrates how widespread and seriously held such beliefs were throughout the Germanic countryside.

Over the years, the motifs of the brutal, bloodthirsty dwarves; the restless, gnawing dead; and even dark witchcraft and sorcery drew together to create strange and malignant vampiric beings. Like many other of its kind, the German/Austrian vampire is a confusing and contradictory figure. Many of the strands of folklore from the dark woods and isolated mountains coalesced into an entity known as an alp.

However, there is no consistency regarding this creature. In parts of Germany, for example, it was a living being—an elemental force such as a gnome or tomtin. In other areas and in Austria, it was the spirit of a dead person that is driven by some malignant impulse. In some areas, it was portrayed as a little old man (a kind of representation of the tomtin). In others, it was a powerful, shapeshifting wizard who went about the countryside in the shape of a cat or a bird. In some areas of Austria, the alp's attacks were of a sexual nature; they leapt upon women and young girls as they slept, like a predator. In this manner, the creature resembled the incubi of ancient Rome. The alp was invariably male and, if it was believed to be the spirit of a deceased person, its attacks were usually directed toward the family that it had left behind. In some instances, it was believed to go about in the guise of a monstrous and extremely lecherous black dog. In this case, it was said, the person had been a werewolf before death, and this linked the notion of the alp into many other folk legends. The connecting feature in all manifestations, however, was that the entity was said to wear some sort of headdress. Usually, this was an old wide-brimmed soft hat, but it could be a covering made of cloth, such as a veil, which obscured most of its face and was possibly used as a disguise.

In the case of a living person who became an alp (and was able to turn into another shape under the influence of the moon), the fault for this always lay with the mother. For example, she had committed some sin during pregnancy that remained unforgiven or she had eaten something (a berry from the bushes, for instance) that was unclean or that the dwarves had spat upon. If "inappropriate measures" had been taken during childbirth (although these were often not specified), the child might grow up to be an alp, or if the mother was frightened by a wild animal—especially a dog or a horse—it would yield the same result. A child born with a caul (a film of thin membrane) across its face might become one of the vampire kind. (Although in other parts of the world, such as Ireland, cauls were considered to be particularly lucky, and a child who was born with one would never be drowned.) Hair on the palm of the hand of an infant might also signal future vampirism; although this could also signal that the child might grow up to become a werewolf. The bodies of small infants were therefore scrupulously studied for some mark or blemish that would give a clue as to their future supernatural destiny.

The Powers of the Alp

In the Brocken and Herz Mountains of Germany, the alp was strongly associated with witchcraft. The mountain region had a dubious supernatural reputation in any case. It was believed that witches gathered amongst the higher peaks in large numbers to create storms and tempests all across the country, and so it seemed natural that they would be connected with the malignant dwarves. The alp, therefore, became the servants and companions of German and Austrian witches and were sent out in the guise of cats or voles in order to work evil in the mountain districts round about.

In Austria and in some parts of Germany, there was an addition to the vampire's powers: alp were able to manipulate the wills of individuals, but only when the people were asleep. The creature had the power to influence their dreams and to create night visions, which would terrify the sleeper beyond measure. The alp could create sleepwalking episodes, fits, and seizures during the night. This they did at the behest of witches and, as such, were associated with the German Mara, a horse-like entity that has given us our word *nightmare*. Indeed, one of its many guises was that of a great white stallion that travelled all through the night-bound countryside, seeking out victims.

The Habergeiss

In addition to the manipulating thoughts and visions, the alp had a liking for both the blood and sometimes the semen of its victims. In some areas of Austria, however, it had a greater liking for the milk of sleeping women and would suck at their breasts until they were sore. There were also variations of the creature in differing regions of the country. For example, in some parts of Austria and in the German mountains, the alp was sometimes known as the *habergeiss*, a creature that reputedly boasted three legs and that, consequently, could move very fast indeed. As soon as darkness had fallen, the habergeiss attacked and drank the blood of cattle grazing in the fields. Normally, it didn't bother with humans unless it was disturbed in its nightly feast, in which case it would attack those who approached it with some ferocity.

The Schrattl

In other parts of the Alp Mountains, the name *schrattl* applied. This referred to a particularly vicious and violent type of vampire, which attacked both humans and animals. This type of vampire had immense mental powers and could render those who it attacked or which it sought influence over, insane. These creatures were not considered to be living things but were considered to be "shroudeaters"—corpses that had come into some form of foul life whilst in the grave and had devoured their way out their winding sheets. In their first instances, both the habergeiss and the schrattl usually attacked members of or property belonging to their own former families, only later broadening their activities to the wider community. Many of these alp are also credited with spreading disease through a region—a common belief concerning vampires everywhere.

Protection Against the Alp

There is no real protection against the alp. In parts of Austria, it was said that the sight of a crucifix or some holy relic would drive them away. Some people therefore tended to wear scapulars or holy medals to ward of their advances, but in the more Protestant regions of Germany this was viewed as superstitious and far too Catholic in tone. In any case, it was countered, these beings were older than Christianity and had been the servants of the very ancient gods that had once dwelt in the deep forests or on the mountainsides. The symbols of the Christian church would therefore have no effect on them. However, salt sprinkled across the doorstep of a house would keep an alp or their kind from entering.

If a community was subject to attacks from the alp, and it was believed that the creature was the spirit of a dead person, then the body had to be rooted out and publicly burned, because this was the only way that it might be destroyed. If the alp was adjudged to be a living person, then that person had to be found and some of their own blood drawn from them, from an area just above the right eye, which would take away their evil powers. Similarly, the "blooding" of a witch who "controlled" the alp would also destroy it and whatever powers it possessed.

Vampire Hysteria

Between 1725 and 1732, some areas of Austria seemed to be gripped by a vampire frenzy. Churchyards were violated as anxious townspeople and villagers sought out the shroudeaters that seemed to be attacking them. Historians seem to suggest that this was the result of some epidemic, such as tuberculosis, but the hysteria was widespread and many bodies were dragged from their coffins and burned. This practice had not abated by 1755 when the town of Olmutz began to

desecrate its cemeteries in the hunt for vampires, which were unsettling the populace. In the German town of Cologne in 1790, an alp in the form of a massive and lascivious dog with red eyes and sparks dropping from the corners of its mouth terrified the population and only disappeared when a certain body was dug up and burned at the municipal cemetery. Even as late as the early 1800s, alps were supposedly drinking blood from the nipples of sleeping men in the Brocken mountain region of Germany, perhaps at the behest of local witches. Cattle and sheep were also attacked but, as far as can be ascertained, no graves were dug up and no bodies burned. Maybe the alp were thought to have been living persons and some other type of communal justice or protection was employed.

The alp is a strange and confusing form of vampire, displaying many peculiar attributes. Sometimes it is the spirit of someone who is dead; sometimes it is an evil manifestation of somebody still alive. Sometimes it takes the form of a small man with a beard and a thirst for blood (representative of the brutal tomtin of former times); in other guises it is a sexual predator or a shapeshifter in the form of an animal, bird, rat, or vole. It drinks blood but it also drinks milk and semen. If the malignant manifestation is of the dead, it can sometimes eat its own shroud and the bodies of those buried close to it. It can sometimes be dispelled by the sight of the Christian cross, but other times and in other regions the holy symbol has no effect on it. Sometimes it even has three legs! This confusion probably reflects a plethora of ancient beliefs concerning both spirits and the dead. The German and Austrian vampire myths have borrowed from a rich vein of traditional folklore, which included elves, dwarves, withes, and werewolves. As well as this, it possibly reflected an earlier time when the countryside was dark and mysterious, swathed in forest and divided by mountains. And yet, who can say that there is not an element of truth in all of this? For who knows what lurks in the woodland glade or along lonely mountain tracks. It is well not to dismiss such old beliefs too lightly. It is well to be careful!

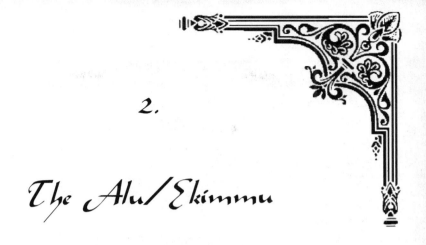

2.

The Alu/Ekimmu

SUMERIA/BABYLONIA

or many ancient peoples, the distinction between vampires and demons was extremely blurred. Demons and devils, it was believed, actually fed and subsisted on human blood and so were drawn to areas of violence whether they were murder sites or battlefields. The spilling of blood was sure to entice them from the shadowy otherworlds where they dwelled. Demons were also credited with the spreading of disease—epidemics and plagues—which, later, was also one of the things connected with vampiric entities. This makes it very difficult to distinguish vampires from other demons. In the ancient Sumerian/Babylonian world the problem was even more complicated by the actual physicality of the vampire.

Ghosts and Spirits

The Sumerians felt that ghosts and spirits were all around them. The spirits were sometimes seen as marauding devils from another world and sometimes as the restless phantoms of the dead who could turn against the living at a moment's notice. These entities manifested themselves in various ways. Sometimes they appeared as a windstorm; sometimes as birds or crawling creatures; sometimes simply as shadows, moving with the sun. Many had been summoned by sorcerers or necromancers for their own evil purposes. The dead were a particular problem, as they could be malicious and violent if they so chose. The ghosts most feared were the shades of those who had died prematurely or in violent circumstances. Thus a person who had been murdered or who had died in an accident was sure to return to torment the living.

Utukku

According to the writer and demonologist Montague Summers, the collective name for wandering spirits was *utukku* (Mesopotamian *uruku*), signifying a type of generalized ghost that was not necessarily hostile. They were rather feeble ghosts, transparent and drifting about in the wind. In the *Epic of Gilgamish*, the hero Gilgamish prays to the god Nergal to restore his dead friend Ea-Bani. The god grants his request and the utukku of Ea-Bani emerges from the earth "like the wind." But it is a transparent and ill-defined shade that speaks with Ea-Bani's voice. The shadow then holds a conversation with Gilgamish. In some commentaries, Ea-Bani is described as a cloud or as a "vague thing—like smoke" and not the sort of entity that would or could harm humans.

Assyrian Ekimmu

In Assyria, however, another, more substantial form of ghost was known. These were the *ekimmu* (sometimes given as *edimmu*). The name literally means "that which is snatched away," signifying that the person concerned had met a violent and untimely death. Exactly what the difference is between utukku and ekimmu is unclear. Summers says there are no discernable differences, but perhaps there *might* have been some fairly basic distinctions.

The Assyrian dead descended into the House of Darkness—a terrible, lightless place, the seat of the god Irkalla, from which those who entered should not come forth again. Their existence there was a rather miserable one—shut away in the darkness and forced to eat dust and mud when they were hungry. But there were those who were not admitted into this bleak Afterworld and who were forced to wander forever through the existence that they had physically left. This, thought the Assyrians, was a much more terrible plight.

Like the Sumerian utukku, these were the ghosts of individuals who had died before their time, but the Assyrians included those who had drowned or who had died in the baking sun of the desert. Indeed, those who had died from dehydration in some barren place were more than likely to be refused entry into the House of Darkness by Irkalla himself, and so they became ekimmu. The refusal of entry made them extremely bad-tempered and violent, and they were liable to turn on the living, whom they envied, and to commit violence against them. The second thing to note was that whereas the utukku were weak, smoky things—more like pathetic, insubstantial revenants—the ekimmu were muscular and wholly solid. This did not, of course, stop them from going about invisibly or from taking other forms, but usually they were substantial physical entities. They tended to dwell in lonely, barren places, well away from the haunts of men. Travellers who passed through these isolated sites—valleys and deserts— were always subject to their attentions.

There was one other fundamental difference: the utukku were generally indifferent spirits, knowing neither good nor

evil. In a number of cases they could be considered benevolent spirits, working with and protecting mankind. In this guise, they were known as *shedu* and might be called upon to protect homes and property. They were usually depicted in early art as winged creatures, usually with the faces of men. In many cases, clay tablets bearing such images—showing the utukku in the form of a lion with a man's head (in this instance they were known as *lamassu*)—were placed on either side of the doorways of houses in order to protect all within. They could also be placed (as statues) at the gates of a city as protectors. There was nothing protective, however, about the ekimmu. They were the implacable enemies of mankind and stopped at nothing to do humans harm.

Traits of the Ekimmu

Descriptions of ekimmu vary from legend to legend. Sometimes they were portrayed as walking corpses, sometimes as winged demons (demonstrating the confusion in the Assyrian/Babylonian mind regarding demons and the dead), sometimes simply as a rushing wind (like a djinn), or sometimes as a shadow moving of its own accord in the midday sun. There was also confusion as to when the ekimmu appeared—some legends say that they were invariably creatures of the night, taking the form of old men and flapping through the darkness on leathery wings; others say they took the form of dust storms that gradually solidified into physical creatures and appeared around midday (like many other ancient peoples, the Assyrians and Babylonians regarded midday, the boundary between morning and evening, with the same sort of dread as they did midnight). Others said they simply took the form of walking corpses and could appear—as did the Greek *vrykolokas*—almost at any time of day, but they especially favored times when the sun was high in the sky. This was when they were at their most dangerous, and travellers should avoid journeying through lonely places at this time even today. Some fables claim that the ekimmu could physically attack passers-by;

other fables say that the ekimmu simply possessed them. The entity was an extremely confusing one.

Gradually, the ways in which a dead person might become an ekimmu began to increase. Previously, only those who had met an unfavorable end were condemned to this state, but now a corpse that had not been buried using proper funerary rites, had been left unburied for too long, or had been left out in the sun might also become one of the walking, violent dead. Furthermore, it was believed that those who died without any relatives to bury them or to tend to their graves might also become ekimmu.

The ekimmu might not necessarily attack a traveller straight away as he crossed some lonely place, but they might attach themselves to him (sometimes invisibly) and follow him home, where they would torment him. Ekimmu might be noisy, poltergeist-like forces, hurling things around the house or breaking artifacts and creating trouble there like an unwelcome guest, or they might, over a period of time, gradually leech away all the victim's energies, leaving him a withered husk and eventually killing him. Once one of these creatures had entered a home or had attached itself to an individual, it was extremely difficult to dislodge and could only be removed by prayer and fasting. It is reported that tales of ekimmu entering houses date back to 2000 or 3000 B.C., making them one of the oldest supernatural entities on record.

The ekimmu took particular forms, and one of the most vicious was the *alu*, or *alus*. Like both utukku and ekimmu, these creatures had died a violent or premature death, but they were particularly hostile toward mankind. Unlike their counterparts, they could not take on a less physically substantial shape, such as wind, dust, or smoke. They were thin and emaciated, their skin was pale to the point of whiteness, and their lips were covered in scabs and blemishes. Of all the Assyrian and Babylonian dead, these were the nearest thing to conventional vampires because they often drank the blood of those

who were dying. Like their counterparts, they usually lived in the wastes and wildernesses, but from time to time they would venture close to a settlement, intending to attack those who lived there. They travelled at night and were often thought to spread disease in their wakes as they went. And, occasionally, house-holders would look up from their evening meals to see the al-most skeletal, disfigured faces of the alu hungrily peering in, yearning for food less wholesome than what was on the table. Sometimes they could be driven away with fire, but a common practice was to distract them with bloody pieces of animal flesh, perhaps from the table. However, there was little protection against them except to wait until they returned to their graves to rest, dig up the bodies, and rebury them with proper funerary practices or else burn them.

Protection Against the Ekimmu/Alu

Few protections against the ekimmu or the alu survive, probably because the Babylonians and Sumerians believed that prevention was better than cure, and so they simply avoided the lonely places where such spirits were said to dwell. It was said, however, that certain magicians or holy men could command them and might offer at least some measure of protection against their machinations. However, such ma-gicians could also bend them to their will, by supernatural means, and use them to terrorize and torment their enemies. In fact, ancient cuneiform (an early form of writing) clay tab-lets containing incantations for raising the dead and turning them into ekimmu are said to exist today, hidden away some-where by scholars, well beyond the reach of laypeople.

Also unearthed by archaeologists are a number of "spirit bowls," which were said to offer protection against the mali-cious and vengeful dead. These are small bowls made from clay and inscribed with certain powerful incantations or spells. The reasoning was that if an exorcist could coax an ekimmu into a dust or spirit form, the creature might be lured under the upturned bowl and become trapped there. However, the upturned bowl could not be lifted or else the ekimmu would be free to terrorize the world once more. Baits could be used to tempt the entity under the bowl: blood or raw meat might be placed there by the magician in order to "draw" the creature there. The spells written on the side of the bowl, it was hoped, might retain the ekimmu there. Similar techniques were later used by sorcerers in ensnaring djinni, and this may form the basis of the popular children's story *Aladdin*, which, although often set in China, has its origins in the Middle East and may originally have been called *El-Haddin*.

The use of magically inscribed bowls, jars, and bottles may have been once thought as a protection against ekimmu and alu but, if there were others, no records of them survive. The main way to dispose of an ekimmu or an alu was to burn its body well away from any human habitation so that the vile spirit might be swept away on the wind. (Several centuries later, in Semitic myth, this element entered the burning of "all that was unclean," which may have included unclean bodies, in the Valley of Hinnom (rendered in Greek as *Gehenna*) outside the City of Jerusalem. Although often described as a "rubbish tip," Hinnom would later become a euphemism for Hell and all its inhabitants. It is also interesting to note that a portion of this valley was called the Aceldama, or Field of Blood, although this is usually understood by Christian theologians to have a connection with the betrayal of Jesus or with the earlier worship of the god Moloch. The valley was certainly a place that the ekimmu and alu would haunt.)

The Semites and Ekimmu/Alu Beliefs

The perceptions of ekimmu and alu were influenced by Semitic beliefs. The Semites believed that such beings were the children of the demoness Lilith and were hostile toward men. They were vile spirits who sought to possess men and

drain their energies. In this, they resembled the Semitic dybbuk. The arrival of the Semitic culture brought the belief that an ekimmu or alu could attach itself to an individual, whether that person was known to it or not, making it a form of demon. However, another name for it—"the leech"—suggests that it was still able to draw off either blood or energy from the individual concerned.

As time went on, Ekimmu began to adopt a wilier approach in their attacks. Rather than simply laying in wait like bandits for travellers to come by and then attack them, they devised tricks and stratagems to lure individuals so that the ekimmu might attach themselves to travellers. A medieval tale from the Middle East illustrated this:

A prosperous wayfarer was passing through a remote part of the country in which there was a particularly fast-flowing river. On its banks, the good-hearted traveller came upon an old, emaciated man who held up thin arms and asked for aid to cross the torrent. He had been sitting there for days, he claimed, waiting on some kind soul who would help him. The traveller took pity on the pathetic old creature and offered to carry him across on his back. He bent down, and the old man gratefully clambered up. They waded out into the river, but as they were halfway across, the withered arms suddenly tightened dangerously around the traveller's throat. In a soft and hissing voice, the ancient informed him that he would never be able to put him down and would be forced to carry him for the rest of his life—if the dreadful creature so desired it. The old man, of course, was an ekimmu. The man returned home with the creature on his back, where it would rest invisibly for the remainder of his days. He had formerly been quite prosperous but, over the years, that prosperity began to slip away and he found himself living in reduced circumstances and on the verge of becoming a beggar. This was put down to the ekimmu "drawing the good" out of everything that he did. In this behavior, the ekimmu acted exactly like a vampire. Eventually the man died, and, as he did so, there was the sound of leathery wings flying away, although nothing was seen. The ekimmu had invisibly departed.

There are other ancient stories of bottles that were opened, releasing their creatures, which then fastened on the individual who had set them free, turning them into virtual slaves. Some of these tales would later translate into Arabic legends concerning djinns and genii.

Concomitant with the belief of the growing powers and craftiness of the ekimmu was a rise in the reliance on various taboos to keep them at bay. Various prohibitions were now brought in to protect individuals against the advances of the ekimmu. Spitting on the ground, for example, was expressly forbidden because it angered the spirits that dwelt there. Those who ate ox meat were susceptible to supernatural attack, as were those who ate pork. This latter prohibition shows the growth of Semitic superstition. For the early Semites, the pig was an "unclean" animal, and to eat its flesh was to invite the attentions of, or possession by, demons and the dead. The best way of eluding ekimmu and alu, however, remained the avoidance of the places where they were to be found (remote valleys and stretches of wasteland). At night, from these spots, the cries and howls of the dead were heard (probably no more than jackals or hyenas), sending a thrill of fear through those who heard them.

Over time, the ekimmu and alu began to merge in the Middle Eastern mind into other equally terrifying creatures of the night—ghouls and efreets. These beings took over from the vampiric ekimmu in their drinking of blood and devouring of flesh. But out in the barren and desert places of the Middle East, who can say what earlier evil still lurks? Under the bloated moon or even in the hot, midday sun, the restless Assyrian dead may still be stirring. Travellers should beware!

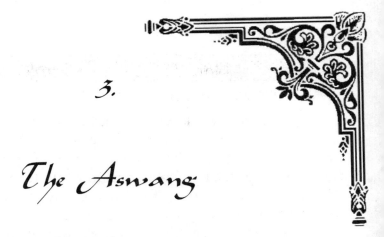

3.

The Aswang

PHILIPPINES

he folklore of the Philippines, especially that which relates to demons and creatures of the night, is extremely difficult and confusing, mainly due to the fact that there are roughly 50 ethnic groups scattered all through the island chain, each with its own belief system. The situation is made even more complex by the existence of several different types of Filipino vampires, and the names are quite often interchangeable from group to group, or even from place to place. This sometimes occurs in East European folklore, but the problem in the Philippines is that such names are often also applicable to both the living and the dead.

The Vampire Witch

Central to many facets of Filipino belief is the idea of the *vampire witch*. This is not one of the dead, but a living woman (or sometimes man) who can transform him or herself in order to do evil against neighbors and to drink their blood or vital fluids. The word *aswang* (the name is said to mean "dog," but it can have a variety of meanings depending on the island or even the district in which it is used) can be applied to these sorcerers whether they are living or dead, for their evil doesn't necessarily end with their demise. In both life and death, they are not altogether human and can change their shape at will. They are most commonly female and they generally attack males. Their favorite victims, however, are small children. They travel about, often in the form of birds, seeking those who are sickly or asleep and therefore unable to defend themselves. Hiding amongst the leaves of nearby trees or somewhere in the eaves of the house, the creature then waits until the victim is alone. From its beak, a long tongue emerges, hollow in the center and extremely sharp at the tip, which it lowers into the room where the individual is lying. Then the creature begins to draw up blood, semen, or sweat through its tongue, which it then drinks.

Many aswang are extremely fond of human blood, which they draw off from a spot on the base of the neck, the upper arm, or the ankle. As the victim loses the blood, so the aswang swells, storing most of the blood in its breasts (it is assumed that most aswang are women), which grow to enormous proportions. Then, heavily laden and gorged with blood, the aswang flies home, where it reverts to human form—usually that of the witch. Her breasts and belly, however, remain swollen with fresh blood (consequently, any big-breasted or heavily built woman was often suspected of being an aswang). She then feeds the blood that she has collected to her own children, in effect making them aswang as well.

Tik-Tik

Just to confuse matters, sometimes, the Filipinos will not refer to this creature as an aswang at all but as a *tik-tik or wak-wak* (which is said to be a *type* of aswang). This is the name of a small owl-like bird that is often found around houses late at night. However, some folklorists state that the tik-tik is *not* an aswang, but the aswang's companion, or else it gives humans warning, with its peculiar cry, that an aswang is near. Even more confusingly, in some parts of the Philippines the tik-tik is said to be an *emanation* of the aswang or the spirit of a living aswang who has died. On the island of Mindanao, this type of aswang is referred to as a *tyanak,* although on many of the other islands the tyanak is the vampiric ghost of a baby who has died without having been baptized.

Traits of the Aswang

In the lore of some islands, the aswang is not a living person at all, but is the corrupted spirit of one who has died violently or in childbirth. In this case, it is a scaly monster, which resembles a flying dragon with a long proboscis, like an anteater has. It is down this nose that the aswang lowers its tongue, thin and pointed like a needle. Flapping on leathery wings, the aswang alights on the roofs of houses where there are young children or someone who is old and feeble. There it waits, seeking out cracks or splits through which it can lower its tongue when the victim is asleep. This type of aswang sleeps during the day and only ventures out after dark.

Yet another type of aswang can split its body, detaching the torso and upper parts from the lower. This is, most assuredly, the sign of a blood-drinking witch. In the Philippines, it is widely believed that the upper body can sprout magical wings and fly about the countryside, doing evil. This type of fiend also has a long, pointed, hollow tongue through which it drinks. Its victims are unborn babies, still in the mother's

womb. Laying the long tongue against the belly of a sleeping, pregnant woman, the aswang draws out the blood and life force from the fetus, causing it to abort or to be stillborn. The rope-like tongue gently "strokes" the edges of the belly without waking the sleeper, allowing the aswang to "drink" from the womb before flying off again to rejoin the lower half of its body. This vampire magician can, however, be thwarted in his or her evil designs. If a good person can find the lower half of the body, which has been abandoned by the sorcerer, he or she must sprinkle salt on it before the upper half returns. This way the two halves of the body cannot reconnect and the aswang torso will eventually shrivel away and die.

Protection Against the Aswang

Salt is considered a protection against aswang of many kinds. In some remote areas, a small bowl of the substance is left near the cribs of sleeping infants to protect them from the creature's attentions. Again, a small bag of salt might be tied around the neck of a child or old person as he slumbers for the same purpose. Sometimes this salt is mixed with human urine, which is believed to be a powerful protective element against the vampire (interestingly enough, this belief is also held is some parts of Eastern Europe). However, in other places, it is believed that salt will not work at all against the aswang and that a combination of certain herbs must be burned within the room next to the sleeper in order to drive the vampire away. Other legends say that salt is only effective against certain *types* of aswang and that the only way to protect oneself is to sleep with a naked blade or an open razor on the chest.

It is worth noting that the aswang against which salt is effective are known as *mannannagel*, which is said to derive from a Filipino word meaning "separate." This bears a close resemblance to a Malay word for vampire—*Pernanggal, Penangllaen,*

or *Penanngallau*—and it may be that the Filipino and Malaysian vampires may have some sort of common, ancestral root belief.

In some communities, aswang are considered to be shapeshifters. This is actually a common characteristic of Filipino witches and ties the notion of the vampire very much to living persons. In this belief system, aswang go about in the guise of cats or small animals, although they may from time to time adopt the larger form of a dog or pig. Again, their favorite victims are either young children or pregnant women, although they have been known to drink the semen of sleeping warriors, thus sapping their strength during the night. These shapeshifters, it is said, are often more likely to be men than women, though this is not always the case. In the case of a male aswang, the favored guise is likely to be that of a fly that buzzes into the house with the intention of seeking out a victim. However, all of these aswang must revert into another form to feed. Sometimes they take on their human form once more; other times they resemble a small, scaly dragon-creature with thin and membranous wings. This being secretes itself amongst the shadows of the house and waits until the victim is asleep. It then scuttles along the walls and lowers its long tongue, gently piercing the skin of the sleeper and drawing up either semen, blood, or visceral fluid. The attentions of the being are totally unknown to the sleeper, who later wakes, feeling weakened and groggy or even nauseous, but is unable to explain why. If the aswang returns on a regular basis, the victim becomes considerably weakened and may eventually die. Consequently, flies are constantly being driven from houses in case they are vampires in disguise.

The Mandurago

Yet another type of aswang, the mandurago, occurs in the folklore of the Tagalog people, who are from a number of

regions in the main island of Luzon. This is an invariably female vampire who is very beautiful and who, though she appears to be alive, may in fact be dead. Her body is then animated by an evil spirit that magically preserves her beauty. This type of aswang will only attack those who are close to it and who may love it, such as suitors or husbands. These people are exceptionally vulnerable to the mandurago's advances, usually at the cost of their own lives. The following Tagalog folktale amply illustrates this vampire at work.

A certain girl was considered one of the most beautiful in her village. She was only 16 years old but had all the attributes of a woman. When she had been about 8 or 9, she had suffered terribly during an epidemic that had swept through the village, and she might well have died except that she was a strong child and managed to make a full recovery. She was much sought after by the young men of the village, who wanted to take her as a wife. But, for a time, she would marry none of them. In the end, she gave in and consented to marry a husky young man, a great warrior and athlete, who had admired her for many years. They lived together in a house at the edge of the village and for a long while appeared very happy. However, people began to notice that the husband was growing pale and was losing some of his virility and strength. Soon after, he sickened with a mysterious illness and died. His widow was as beautiful as ever, and, after a decent period, other men in the village—former suitors that she'd rejected—began to court her again. She married once more; this time to a warrior who was as husky and strong as her first husband had been. Shortly after marriage, however, he too seemed to be failing. He became thin and pale, and seemed much weaker than before. His condition lasted for just over a year before he too died. Conversely, she remained positively radiant. There was now great suspicion throughout the village, that his wife had somehow poisoned him but noone said anything, as the girl

came from a good and respected family. All the same, the girl seemed to grow more beautiful as time passed, and it was known that she was intending to marry again. However, her suitors were not so numerous now; the young men of the village began to fear her. One man, nevertheless, said that he would marry her, and so he did—but he was wary of her. He went to bed on the first night after their wedding and feigned sleep. Soon he felt something like a rope stealthily moving across his body, and he guessed that this was the long tongue of the aswang. Turning over in the bed, he saw that it was not a beautiful girl who lay beside him but a long, lizard-like thing with a long nose like an anteater from which a long and barbed-looking tongue protruded. Reaching under the bed, he drew out a knife that he had placed there earlier and struck out at the thing. It was difficult to see the creature, but he felt the blade sink into something and he heard a loud scream like that of a night bird somewhere close by. This was followed by a sustained flapping noise as the creature made its escape. After lighting a lamp, he saw that the bed was covered in a greenish ichorous substance, which he assumed was the blood of the aswang. Some time after, the body of the young girl was found deep in the forest; she appeared quite dead. But was this a real body or simply a husk that had been occupied by a mandurago, the village elders asked. It was thought that the girl had *already* died during the epidemic when she was 8 and that for the remainder of her years had been an aswang.

A similar Tagalog story concerns a strong and vigorous young man who lived on the edge of a forest.

Deep among the trees, an old beggar woman was living in a rude and almost derelict hut. She was very old—nobody could say how old she was for she seemed to have lived there forever—and she was rumoured to be a witch. Locals were

said to visit her under the cover of darkness for healing powders and love potions. The young man himself, as far as was known, had nothing at all to do with her and yet, in the evening, she would be seen skulking through the undergrowth, not too far from his home. He began to waste away and his strength began to fail. His family was puzzled, but those who knew suspected that it might be due to the work of an aswang, so a couple of them laid a trap for the creature.

One night the young man retired to bed, sleeping just below the window that looked out into the forest while his friends waited in the shadows. After some time there was a rustling on the other side of the open window as if somebody or something was creeping close to the house. Something curled itself over the window ledge, toward the sleeping man. At first, it looked like a snake, but the watchers soon realized that it was the tongue of an aswang, studded with tiny barbs to draw blood and vital fluids from the sleeping man. The people attacked the thing with a metal knife, and there was a scream from somewhere outside the house. Looking out, they saw a bizarre creature sitting on the ground just outside the building. It had the long, scaled body of a reptile and small leathery wings, but it also had the human head of the old lady who lived in the forest. Her mouth was open and the studded tongue protruded from it, extending all the way across the ground and through the window. The tip of the tongue was as sharp as a blade. One of the men threw glowing coals at the thing, and with another shriek it drew back into the forest, flapping its way between the trees. They followed it to the hovel and there they found the old woman lying dead with her natural tongue extended. The young man recovered and soon regained full health and strength. There was no doubt that the crone had been an aswang, spreading evil and disease through the villages all about.

The aswang is probably one of the most complex and contradictory vampire figures. It is also one of the most fascinating; its variations reflect the rich tapestry of cultures that make up the Philippines. The forests and jungles on the various islands hide a variety of strange and mystifying secrets—secrets that are only whispered about by those who live there. And who is to say that the vampiric aswang is not one of them?

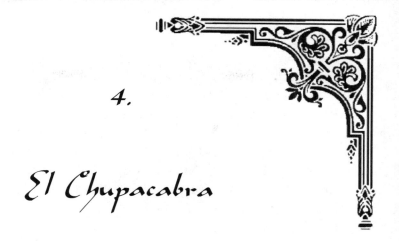

4.

El Chupacabra

PUERTO RICO/MEXICO

omewhere between the San Pedro River and the southern tip of the Huachuca Mountains in southwestern
Arizona, the army of Francisco Vazquez de Coronado
made camp. It was April 1540, and the governor of New Galicia
was leading an expedition comprised of mounted *conquista-
dors*, foot soldiers, and a large herd of livestock across the northern borders of the Spanish lands and into unknown territory
that would later become the states of Arizona and New Mexico.
He was seeking the fabled Seven Cities of Cibola, the cities of
gold, which his informant, the priest Fray Marcos de Niza,
assured him lay somewhere in the wilderness. His expedition was doomed to failure. He was not destined to find the
cities of gold, only the mud pueblos of local Indians, but
perhaps he had the first encounter with something even more
intriguing.

A legend says that as he camped during the night, Coronado's livestock were attacked. It is told that some of his men drove off the attackers—described as small, dark, horny-skinned men—with torches and spears. In the morning, many of the cattle, which made up the main herd (1,500 animals), were dead, drained of blood. Despite this setback, Coronado was able to buy cattle from local Indians, replacing most of those that he'd lost, and press onward in his quest.

In the Zuni Indian pueblo at Hawikuh in Western New Mexico, he heard tales of strange grey men with "knives on their backs" who had sporadically fought with the Zunis in times long past. They could jump, the Zunis told him, over long distances and drop off their warriors from above, killing them with pointed sticks. It was said, the Zunis went on, that they drank blood. These tales were of little interest to Coronado, as his destination was the legendary Cibola, and all this talk of ferocious dwarves was only a distraction. His disdain and arrogance inflamed the Zunis, and they attacked him and provoked a minor battle, at which the Indians were defeated.

In the spring of 1541, having crossed the Witchita River in search of a legendary city named Quivara and finding only the grass-covered villages of the Witchita Indians, Coronado finally turned back. He returned to Mexico City in 1542 broken and defeated, with most of his army lost to Indians and disease. At this time, all thoughts of those tiny blood-drinking attackers must have been very far from his mind (he had dismissed the attackers as Indians anyway), and the mystery would lie dormant for more than 400 years when it would resurface many miles away.

The Reemergence of el Chupacabra

During the hot summer of 1975, several farm animals in the Puerto Rican mountains were found dead and completely drained of blood. For a long time—nearly 100 years—there had been tales of queer little men who lived somewhere deep in the hills and who subsisted on blood—mainly the blood of goats kept by mountain farmers. For this reason, the creatures were known as *el chupacabra*, "goat-suckers," although it was unclear whether they were actually another species of man or some previously unknown form of animal. The animals found in 1975 had small puncture marks on their necks, and there seemed little doubt in the local community that this was the work of el chupacabra.

Traits of el Chupacabra

In the realms of vampirology, the chupacabra is something of an enigma. It is not clear exactly what sort of being it might be. Is it, for example, a dead soul that has somehow taken physical form? There have been suggestions that it is some form of unidentified marsupial and therefore belongs in the realm of cryptozoology. There have even been suggestions that it might be something extraterrestrial—something from beyond the stars.

A number of photos have appeared over recent years, each purporting to be a true likeness of the creature, but each of these is open to question. A number have been dismissed as deliberate fakes.

Descriptions of the creature abound, all of which are fairly consistent, and so it's possible to build up some kind of picture of the chupacabra. It is said to be roughly 3 to 5 feet tall with dark grey facial skin. Coarse hair covers its body and some legends say that it has the power to change color (like a chameleon). Its eyes are black though sometimes they can appear yellow or red and are said to glow in the dark. Some descriptions portray it with a canine-like snout and ears depressed against the side of its head like a wolf. Its teeth are sharp—the incisors are almost fangs—and are said to be

hollow. It is sometimes thought these that the chupacabra draws up and stores the blood from its victims. The creature has short forearms that end in three-fingered claw-like "hands," capable of tearing into flesh. It has a row of fins, spikes, needles, or quills running down its back, possibly for the length of its spine (these may be the "knives" that the Zuni Indians described to Coronado). The chupacabra stands upright like a man on two extremely powerful hind legs that end in clawed feet.

Some descriptions say that it could fly on thin, bat-like wings; others state that it travels by leaping into the air (one witness describes it leaping as high as twenty feet in a single bound) and that it makes a hissing noise that frightens everyone. It leaps upon its prey with a single bound, sinking its teeth into the base of their necks and drawing out blood. Some witnesses say that it can discharge venom if disturbed. When moving toward its victim, el chupacabra walks upright on its hind legs like a man.

Between the first attacks in 1975 and 1991, the creature's appetite seemed to grow. Animals, particularly sheep and goats, were often found dead all across the Puerto Rican mountains. In 1995, Luis Guadalupe, a hill farmer who had seen the creature attack some of his livestock, told a local newspaper that it was "like an ugly dwarf" and that it appeared to have "a pointy, long tongue like a snake." As he approached, it hissed at him with a sound that made him feel nauseous, and it jumped away with massive bounds, which made the farmer think that it might be flying. Another witness, Madelyne Tolentino, claimed that it "jumped like a kangaroo" on powerful hind legs, hissing and spitting as it went, and that there was a peculiar smell in the air as it passed—"like sulphur." Other witnesses said that el chupacabra had "supernatural strength" and was able to carry off a full-grown cow into some rocks where it drank the animal's blood.

By the late 1990s, however, subtle differences began to emerge in the descriptions of the creature compared to those that had been given earlier. Its "face" was less wolf-like and more like that of a ram; it had long, thin wings wrapped around it like a cloak; it could run along the ground, upright like a man but faster than a galloping horse; it had the ability to breathe fire if disturbed in its activities; its hands were more "monkey-like" than clawed; it had an alligator-like skin. Some of these additions were probably no more than the imagination of local Puerto Rican farmers, but it is worthy of note that the basic descriptions of the being remain the same throughout all the tales.

Early in 1991, a number of dogs were found on the mountain farms. Not only was their blood gone, but their insides were also sucked out by some unknown creature. In the minds of the farmers this was indisputable evidence of el chupacabra, and it also served to prove, in the popular mind at least, that they were growing hungrier. "The carcases were like discarded rags," the report stated. "As though everything had been sucked out of them through the eyes. Internal organs— heart, liver, stomach—were all gone."

El Chupacabra Beyond Mexico

For a time, the carnage seemed to be confined to the island of Puerto Rico, but toward the late 1990s, other Caribbean islands began to report similar outrages, and there were several sightings of the beasts—if beasts they were—in Mexico, Chile, and even in some of the southern U.S. states such as Arizona and Texas. Whole packs of stray dogs were found dead over large areas of Texas—some drained of blood, others without any internal organs. Livestock in both Texas and Arizona were attacked and killed, tiny puncture marks found in their necks. Dogs and sheep have been attacked in northern Florida and cattle have been savaged in Baja, California. But for all its

ferocity and audacity, el chupacabra has not, so far, been known to attack human beings.

Debating el Chupacabra's Existence

But the question still persists: what is the thing? In Puerto Rico, the theory was advanced amongst the hill people that chupacabras were the souls of evil men who had come back in the form of ugly dwarves in order to torment the living and to wreak revenge for past insults. This is considered as a folkloric explanation and one that falls within the realm of ghosts and demons to which the more conventional vampires belong. Another, more "scientific" answer that has been put forward is that it might be a type of dinosaur that has somehow survived since earliest times and has remained undetected until now. Still others put it down as some form of exotic animal that had initially been illegally imported to Puerto Rico and has managed to reproduce itself. All sources agree, however, that the creature is vampiric and that it needs blood in order to sustain itself. It is also, apparently, somewhat afraid of humans, and it tries to avoid them.

A number of attempts have been made by authorities to deny that el chupacabra actually exists. The former director of Puerto Rico's Department of Agriculture's Veterinary Division, Hector Garcia, issued a statement saying that there was actually nothing unusual about the killings, which were observed during his period of office, and other government officials have blamed the deaths on marauding feral panthers. Still others have even blamed the deaths on human beings who might have carried them out for occult purposes. But *Fate* magazine has suggested that they are taking chupacabras much more seriously than they are formally stating, particularly in the southern United States.

ABEs

There are hints that the vampire-creature has been given a specific scientific designation, *Anomalous Biological Entities* (ABEs), and that a special taskforce comprised of scientists operating in southwestern Texas during 2000 and 2001 was set up to tackle them. In fact, there have been numerous attempts to link ABEs (and specifically el chupacabra) with either UFOs or secret U.S. biological experiments. Those who believe that the entity is an ABE are further convinced of a deliberate U.S. government and media conspiracy to keep it from public attention, perhaps to prevent widespread panic. Several attempts by the government of Puerto Rico to initiate public enquiries into the entire chupacabra belief have all come to nothing.

In 2000–2001, a team from the *Inside Edition* program travelled to Puerto Rico to investigate the story from an ABE angle. It has been suggested that their report was not entirely unbiased and that they were actually sent in order to ridicule the story to the public, as the program virtually dismissed the whole idea as fantasy. The program allegedly mocked the whole idea of the chupacabra and ridiculed the mayor of Canavanas, who was one of the supposed witnesses to an attack. Although there were several stories that U.S. Marines and a unit of the Puerto Rican army had captured two of the creatures and were holding them somewhere in the United States, these claims were dismissed out of hand by the makers of the program, and any witnesses were portrayed as unreliable.

The source of this assertion, however, is a Puerto Rican journalist name Jorge Martin whom U.S. agencies have described as being "completely untrustworthy." Martin himself seems to favor what he terms as "genetic manipulations," which have produced a vampire-creature. He draws attention to the work of several genetic scientists such as one whom he names as Dr. Tsian Kanchen, a Chinese-Russian genetic

scientist who allegedly worked for the former Soviet Union. According to Martin, Kanchen had produced certain "genetic manipulations" under laboratory conditions and may have created a new species of electronically crossed plant and animal hybrids. Using an electronic system that could pick out what Martin describes as "certain bioenergetic signatures" from bio-organisms at a DNA level and could then electronically transfer them to other species, he had, Martin suggests, created incredible new types of chicken and ducks, which manifested characteristics of both species; as well as goats and rabbits and cereal crops. He was, it is claimed, one of the forerunners of the current genetic modification in crops.

It is further thought that shortly before the collapse of the USSR, Kanchen defected to the West, taking his technology with him, where he offered his services to the United States. Martin suggests that even if he didn't defect and if the Soviet Union was undertaking such genetic experiments, then the United States was probably conducting them too.

He also revealed that one of the chupacabras had been shot and wounded by a farmer in the Puerto Rican highlands but that it had fled, leaving a trail of its own blood behind. The blood, he reports, was subsequently taken away and examined by a team from both the Puerto Rican and U.S. authorities. Martin claims to have had access to a copy of the results of their analysis, which, he claims, was in no way compatible with normal human blood. The trace ratio of magnesium, he says, together with those of phosphorous, calcium, and potassium were far higher than those found in the blood of humans. The albumen/glouline (RG ratio) is also vastly different. Nor are the results compatible with any known animal species, Martin asserts. The team who investigated it declared the blood to be from a creature not native to Earth, or so Martin says.

The U.S. and Puerto Rican authorities, however, dismiss his claims out of hand, saying that they are totally spurious: there never has been a scientific defector named Tsian Kanchen, and the whole story is "utterly fantastic and worthy of cheap science fiction." The authorities also point out that no research was ever carried out into alleged chupacabra blood and that Martin has made the whole thing up himself.

All the same, alleged sightings of el chupacabra continue to grow over an increasingly wider area. The creature and its work have been reported all over Texas and in a growing area in northern Florida, as well as in Chile and Brazil. Between 1999 and 2003, cattle mutilations in these areas have greatly increased. All the dead animals have been drained of their blood and have tiny puncture marks at the base of their necks. The deaths have restarted speculation about biological mutations and creatures from beyond the stars.

However, none of this theory explains what the Zuni Indians told Coronado, far back in the 16th century. They spoke of "devil men," ugly dwarves who lived in the hills and attacked both them and their herds with a terrible ferocity. They spoke of deformed little men who drank the blood of the fallen. They spoke of vampires. Coronado ignored these tales, but they were perhaps the first hints at a great mystery that has maybe lasted for at least 400 years—a mystery that is still with us.

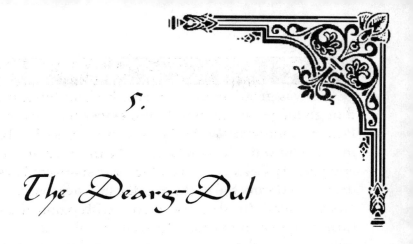

5.

The Dearg-Dul

IRELAND

It may come as a surprise to some, but Dracula's home may be in Ireland. In light of prevalent mythology, which connects the vampire count with Transylvania, it is sometimes easy to forget that the man who wrote the novel, Abraham (Bram) Stoker, was in fact Irish and had been influenced by Irish folklore. It is also easy to forget that one of the earliest written accounts of vampires came from Ireland.

In many respects, Stoker's novel *Dracula* (published in 1897) reflects 19th-century Ireland a little more than it does Eastern Europe (an area that Stoker had never visited and only knew about from travel writers). The roadside shrines, the dark woods, the small villages full of superstitious peasants, all reflect the Ireland of the mid-1800s, an Ireland with which Stoker might have been vaguely familiar.

He was growing up in interesting and brooding times. Although too young himself to remember the horrors of the Irish Potato Famine (1845–1852) he would probably have known many who did. He would have heard how, in County Clare and County Galway (some of the worst affected areas), people drew blood from the necks of cattle in order to make the ghastly "relish cakes" (fresh blood mixed with oatmeal and greens—turnip tops or rotted cabbage stalks) and baked into tiny cakes that were used to assuage the awful hunger in the country areas as subsequent potato crops failed. He may have heard, too, how starving villagers may even have drunk blood directly from the veins of cattle and horses or bit the heads off chickens in order to gain what nourishment they could. In Counties Roscommon and Mayo, the starving people were said to drink the blood of domesticated dogs, whilst in County Leitrim a man tried to drink the blood of a wild fox and was rewarded by losing his right arm to the animal's jaws. Bloodletting and the drinking of blood were fast becoming features of Irish rural life around this time, and many of the areas where this occurred still bear the memory in the placenames (designated community sites where animal blood was let).

Stoker also might have heard tales of the epidemics that swept through parts of Ireland during the early-to-mid 19th century. Cholera and typhoid swept across great swathes of the country, bringing a protracted and lingering death to many. Stoker's mother came from County Sligo, which, during the late 1700s and early 1800s, had experienced serious epidemics of tuberculosis, and the young Abraham may have heard stories of a ghastly disease that turned the skin pale as marble and caused its victims to cough up blood. At the height of the epidemic, whole villages were infected and local churchyards were filled with infected corpses.

Both famine and plague produced their own folklore. It was said that after the Potato Famine had passed, some of those who had tasted blood had become addicted to it and secretly continued to drink it—in effect, becoming human vampires. The Fir Gorta (the Man of Hunger), an emaciated creature somewhere between a spectre and a fairy, tramped the Irish roads with a staff in one hand and a small metal begging cup in the other. At the back door of the houses it passed, it would rattle the cup and make a faint call for alms. If those in the house ignored the sound and did not leave a coin or a piece of food by the back door for him, sickness and perhaps death would descend upon them. At this time, too, the Dullahan, an awful headless horseman, thundered over the nightbound Irish countryside, with disease under his cloak, infecting the households he passed. Such tales kept memories of plagues and of the Potato Famine very much alive in the Irish mind.

Legend of Carrickaphouka Castle

But there were other, older legends that concerned members of the Gaelic aristocracy. In 1601, for instance, Cormac Tadhg McCarthy of Carrigphouka Castle near Macroom, County Cork, was made high sheriff of the entire county. Carrickaphouka itself had a sinister reputation. The name means "the rock of the pouka"—the pouka, or pooka, being a type of demon that terrorized many places in Ireland. Sometimes, it appeared as a great horse; sometimes, as an eagle; and sometimes, as a feral goat with long, curling horns. Often it was too terrible to describe. The rock on which the McCarthy castle stood was supposed to be inhabited by one such being and its malignant character was said to have been reflected in its chief inhabitant.

Cormac Tadhg McCarthy was said to have been a fierce, brooding man, but he was greatly favored by the English, who were trying to subdue the lands around Cork. With their help, and in his new role of high sheriff, he began to hunt down many of the rebels who were opposing English rule. One of the best known of these rebels was James Fitzgerald, who had rallied a substantial band of disaffected Irish lords. On the pretext of making peace, Cormac McCarthy invited Fitzgerald to a banquet in Carrickaphouka, where he poisoned him. Not content with merely killing Fitzgerald, and to show his loyalty to his English masters, the sheriff had him cooked, and he ate his flesh and drank his blood in front of them. The act shocked and horrified all of Ireland and blackened the McCarthy name for many centuries. The clan itself tried to excuse Cormac's cannibalistic behavior by saying that he had been possessed by the spirit of the pouka that dwelt in the rock. However, the body of the evil sheriff was said to return to the castle (now a ruin—destroyed during the Williamite Wars in Ireland), animated by dark forces, in order to attack and drink the blood of passers-by—becoming, in effect, a vampire. The fallen castle lies two miles west of the town of

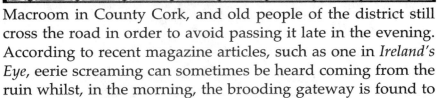

Macroom in County Cork, and old people of the district still cross the road in order to avoid passing it late in the evening. According to recent magazine articles, such as one in *Ireland's Eye*, eerie screaming can sometimes be heard coming from the ruin whilst, in the morning, the brooding gateway is found to be splattered with fresh blood.

Writing about Carrickaphouka, the *Irish Monthly* (1874) used the term *derrick-dally* for the apparition that was said to haunt it. The word *derrick-dally* is probably an Anglicized corruption of the ancient Irish name for such ghosts (*dearg-dulai* or *dearg-dul*). The exact meaning of this term is unclear (several folklorists have translated it as "red blood-sucker"), but it is usually taken to mean "one who drinks blood." For the ancient Celts, as with many other ancient warrior peoples, blood was the symbol of life; it was the very essence of a person—the source of his wisdom, skill, and strength. There is evidence to suggest that, after a battle, Celtic warriors may have smeared themselves in the blood of their dead enemies in order to gain some of their powers and prowess, whilst the barbaric European Huns actually shed blood as a sign of mourning at the grave of a recently deceased chieftain so he might take something of them with him into the next world. It was said that at the funeral of Attila, more than 400 Hun warriors slit veins in their arms and that some died as a result, leading to a papal ban against the practice amongst warrior races. And yet, the blood motif continued, often referring to great warrior chieftains and the notion of drinking their blood in order to imbibe some of their greatness. This may have given rise to the notion of the dearg-dul.

Tale of Leap Castle

Another blood-drinking Irish spectre is that of Tadhg O'Carroll, former owner of Leap Castle in southern Offaly. Like Carrickaphouka, the castle itself has a sinister reputation. Its

rather peculiar name comes from the ancient Irish *Leim ui Bhanain* (the leap of the O'Bannions), which, in turn, has its source in a particularly blood-soaked legend.

Driven south from the lands around northern County Monaghan by an expansion of the O'Neills around the 12th and 13th centuries, the O'Carrolls (a fierce and cruel sept) settled in the ancient kingdom of Ely, which stretched right across Offaly and part of North Tipperary. These lands were already inhabited by a number of other clans, one of which was the O'Bannions. The O'Carrolls set about subduing these other clans by the sword, quickly becoming masters of most of the kingdom. The O'Bannions, however, held out, and, in an attempt to resolve the situation, a peculiar compromise was reached. Near the site of an ancient Christian foundation at Sier Kieron (between Kinnity and Rosscrea) stood two great rocks some distance apart. If an O'Bannion champion could jump between them and survive, his clan could retain its lands; if not, it passed into the hands of the O'Carrolls. The leap was made, but the champion fell short of the stone and was dashed to pieces on the ground below them. To commemorate the O'Carroll "victory," a castle was erected on the spot; the stones of its foundation were held together by mortar mixed with the blood of the fallen O'Bannion champion. This castle—Leap— was to become one of the foremost O'Carroll fortifications, guarding a main trail through the Slieve Bloom Mountains that linked the coast with the plain of Leix and Offaly. But it was always reputedly cursed (the words of the curse being "Raised in blood; blood be its portion") and many of the O'Carrolls died there, some in allegedly mysterious circumstances.

In the early-to-mid 1500s, the kingdom of Ely and the O'Carrolls themselves were badly divided. The kingdom had become a buffer zone in a conflict that raged right across the Irish midlands between the pro-English Butlers (the Dukes of Ormond and North Tipperary) and the Gaelic Fitzgeralds (the Earls of Desmond and Kildare). The wily O'Carrolls played

one side against the other, firstly leaguing with the Butlers, and then with the Fitzgeralds. But, gradually, the clan itself began to split and, in the early 1500s, two leaders had emerged, each controlling a faction of the clan. These were One-Eyed Tadhg of Leap Castle and his cousin Calvagh, who hated each other. Tadhg assumed a kind of temporary chieftainship of the entire clan around 1541, but his chieftainship was always hotly disputed. The actual clan chief should have been Tadhg's elder brother, Thaddeus MacFir, but he was declared "incompetent" due to the fact that he was a priest.

Tadhg decided to back the Butlers and made a treaty with the Duke of Ormond, James the Lame, who was backed by the English. However, at every turn he found himself thwarted by his elder brother who, though a cleric, still dabbled in politics. Thaddeus struck a deal with the Fitzgeralds that undermined most of Tadhg's plans. His one-eyed brother fumed and swore vengeance. According to legend, he invited Thaddeus, in his official role as priest, to come and say Mass at Leap. The castle chapel lay at the very top of the central tower and, while Thaddeus knelt across its altar rails in prayer, Tadgh came up behind him and cut his throat. This was not only an act of murder, it was an act of blasphemy because Thaddeus had been speaking directly to God. It meant that the chapel was not used as such again, but became a banqueting place. Here Tadhg had an oubliette installed. This was a fearsome drop, like a dumbwaiter that fell all the way to the base of the tower. Into this enemies were thrown and then bricked in and forgotten about (the name *oubliette* comes from the French *oublier*—"to forget"). It is said that at the height of his powers in the area, Tadhg threw about 40 of the O'Mahons (another enemy clan whom he'd invited to a banquet, once again, on the pretext of making peace) into the oubliette and sealed them there.

In 1552, Tadhg made peace with the English and accepted a knighthood. This antagonized several of his brothers who,

urged on by his enemy, Calvagh, attacked and murdered Tadhg, bringing to an end his bloody overlordship of the clan. In 1688, the O'Carrolls finally left the area in return for a grant from the English of 60,000 acres of land in Maryland in the Americas. Leap Castle was given to the English Darby family, but their stay there was unsettled. Today, the castle enjoys the dubious reputation of being the most haunted site in Western Europe.

Amongst the ghosts that haunt the place is that of Tadhg O'Carroll. Because he had committed a blasphemous act by slaying his brother whilst in communication with God, his soul was damned and was denied entrance into Heaven. Therefore, according to popular belief, it was confined to the place in which he had committed his blasphemous act, now known as "The Bloody Chapel," condemned to subsist upon the blood of those who ventured into it. Much of Leap Castle was burned during the Irish Civil War, and today only a part of it has been restored. The Chapel is now little more than an empty smoke-blackened chamber, but it still has an eerie feel to it. Perhaps it is the glassless windows, through which birds come and go, but even on the warmest days, the place still boasts a certain unaccountable chill.

The Marbh Bheo

Both Tadhg O'Carroll and Cormac Tadhg McCarthy are counted among what the Irish have called the *marbh bheo* — the night-walking dead. The imminence of the dead was at one time felt everywhere in Ireland, and this is reflected in many placenames throughout the country. There is a tale of a blood-drinking fairy or corpse that haunts the road between Dun Chaoin (Dunquinn) and Baile Feirtearaigh (Ballyferriter) on the Dingle Peninsula in County Kerry. The dearg-dul is said to be particularly active along a stretch of roadway near a place known as Casadh na Graise, where two streams meet. In County Galway, the area of Glan na Scail is taken to mean "the valley of the phantom" or "dark supernatural being." The place is reputedly badly haunted and was shunned by travellers in olden days. Drumarraght, near Maguiresbridge in County Fermanagh, is taken to mean "the ridge of apparition," though all inquiries as to how it acquired its name have come to naught. And yet, the placename is suggestive of a ghost or phantom, as is the name Drumadarragh (Anglicized into Drumadraw), a site near Coleraine in County Derry. Anascaul in County Kerry is actually Abhain na Scail, "the river of the phantom." Glengesh in County Donegal actually means "the taboo valley," and it is generally accepted in this locality that the taboo has something to do with the walking dead who are said to haunt the valley. All of these sites, and many others, are linked to the notion of the returning dead—a motif that played a significant part in the early Celtic psyche.

There was also the idea of blood-drinking fairies and flesh-eating cadavers, or those who had been "touched" by the fairy kind to become a sort of ravening monster in their own right. In the late 1930s, a recorder for the Irish Folklore Commission, Tim Murphy, travelled through the wilds of County Kerry, formally collecting horrific stories of girls who had unwittingly married corpses and of ghoulish practices in isolated churchyards. In the remote parish of Sneem, Murphy heard tales of women who, late at night, left the sides of their sleeping husbands to devour the flesh and drink the blood of newly interred corpses. He also heard of fairies, in the far hills, that would attack travellers in order to suck the blood from their arms and legs. Indeed, there were said to be whole forts of them living somewhere amongst the Kerry mountains. At a lecture given at University College, Dublin, in 1961, the archivist of the Irish Folklore Commission, Sean O'Suilleabhain (a Kerryman), spoke of such a fortress high in the Macgillycuddy's Reeks mountain range. It guarded, he said, a lonely pass between two peaks (although he didn't name them) and the inhabitants preyed on lone travellers passing

through. The beings who dwelt there, described by O'Suilleabhain as *neamh-marbh* (the Undead), were most assuredly vampires. Unfortunately, he gave no clue as to the location of this fortress—simply saying that it was "an old Kerry folktale"—and so there is no way of tracking where it might be. He referred to the fort as *Dun dreach-fhoula* (translated as the "castle of the blood-visage") and no maps of the area reveal such a place. And yet, tales of blood-drinking fairies and spectres exist all over Ireland in remote and geographically isolated areas such as the Macgillycuddy's Reeks.

The Tale of Abhartach

These stories and legends may have been familiar to Stoker and may well have formed at least part of the idea for Dracula. But there was also another tale—even older—that may have influenced him as well. This was the tale of the ancient Celtic warlord Abhartach, which, as far as we know, is the oldest formally recorded vampire story in Western Europe.

The legend comes from the townland of Slaughtaverty, near the town of Garvagh in North Derry, which, though it is only a few miles from the town, is still a fairly isolated spot. It lies in the Glenullin valley and is cut off on three sides by the beginning of the Sperrins mountain range. In the fifth and sixth centuries, this valley was a patchwork of tiny kingdoms, each ruled by individual "kings" who were little more than local warlords.

Abhartach was one of these warlords and very little is known about him. However, tradition suggests that he may have been small in stature or deformed in some way, but that he was certainly a most powerful wizard. He was also a tyrant, mercilessly ruling his people.

Those under the harsh rulership of Abhartach wished to get rid of him, but because of his dark powers they were too frightened to attack him themselves. So they hired another chieftain called Cathan, or Cathain, to come and kill him for them, which he did, slaying Abhartach and burying him standing up, a befitting burial for an Irish chieftain. The next day, however, Abhartach was back, demanding a basin filled with blood from the wrists of his subjects, in order, says the legend, "to sustain his vile corpse." Cathan came and slew him again and buried him in the same place. The next day the ghastly cadaver came back again with the same grisly demand. Puzzled, Cathan went either to the druids or to a holy man who lived in nearby Gortnamoyagh Forest and asked him the reason for this puzzling supernatural phenomenon. The holy man thought for a moment.

"The evil Abhartach is not dead," he replied at length. "But he is in a state of suspension due to his dark arts. He has become one of the *neamh-marbh* and cannot, therefore, be killed. But he can be prevented from rising again." In order to do this, the hermit told him, Cathan must "slay" Abhartach with a sword made of yew wood; he must bury him upside down; he must surround the gravesite with thorns; and he must place a great stone directly above the spot where the vampire lay. All this Cathan did, even going so far as to create a great "leacht," or sepulchre over the creature. This gave the townland its name: Slaughtaverty, or Abhartach's leacht. The grave is still there; now in the middle of a wide barley field. It is said that the thorns that Cathan placed around the site have grown together into a thorn tree that grows above the remnants of the sepulchre (although the tree there is of much more recent date). A massive stone from the now-fallen tomb lies above the place where Abhartach is said to lie. Even today, local people will not approach the field after nightfall.

The legend of Abhartach was recorded as actual history by Seathrun Ceitinn's (Dr. Geoffrey Keating) *Foras Feasa na Eireann*

(*The History of Ireland*), written between 1629 and 1631. It was translated by a number of scholars, including Dermod O'Connor, and was later enthusiastically recounted by Patrick Weston Joyce in his *General History of Ireland*. It was widely told all over Ireland, and it may have been that Stoker heard it on one of his visits to Sir William and Lady Wilde (the parents of Oscar Wilde), who were his friends. He certainly knew of Dr. Keating's book. Trinity College in Dublin (where Bram Stoker lived) possessed two copies of it, one of which was briefly put on display. The display chapter was Keating's treatise on the *neamh-marbh*. Whilst there is absolutely no evidence that Stoker himself could either speak or read the Irish language, in which the text was written, he had many friends who could, so the significance of the section was not lost on him. The Irish warlord Abhartach may have been partly responsible for the Transylvanian count.

Other Irish Folklorists

Stoker, of course, was not the only Irishman to write about vampires and the walking dead. In 1872, Joseph Sheridan Le Fanu (1814–1873) had published an anthology that contained the eerie vampire story "Carmilla," also set in Eastern Europe, and another of his collections included the tale of "Shalken the Painter," in which a beautiful young girl marries an animated, decaying corpse. As did Stoker, Le Fanu drew upon Irish folklore for his inspiration. He was undoubtedly influenced by the legends of the Undead Earl of Desmond who rose from his tomb beneath the waters of Lough Gur in County Limerick to ride around the surrounding district, carrying off young men or young women to lie with him in his watery grave, or the myriad stories of girls who fell in love with mysterious strangers only to find that they were the Undead.

Following in the same tradition, folklorists such as the American Jeremiah Curtin (1835–1906) collected Irish stories

of malignant corpses who caught those who passed by their resting places, climbed upon their backs, and were carried about all through the hours of darkness. One in particular, "The Blood-drawing Ghost," in which a young girl carries a murderous cadaver into a house in order that it might cut the throats of the sleepers there, is especially resonant of the vampire myth. Similar stories are found across the island, from Limerick to Leitrim, all telling of the malicious dead who lurked in the shadows with a hostile intent toward the living.

Ireland, then, may not be as charming and pleasant as it first seems. Beneath the surface of Irish folklore—long equated with shamrocks and leprechauns—lies a dark strand concerning the watching dead. It is a brave man or woman who will venture out along a lonely Irish road, where old churchyards and falling Great Famine villages nestle amongst the far-off trees, as twilight falls across the countryside. Who knows what he or she may encounter before reaching his or her destination. Dark, blood-drinking fairies or the malignant *marbh-bheo*, hungry for fresh human flesh? The ravening ghosts of Cormac McCarthy or Tadhg O'Carroll? Or, even worse, the unquiet shade of Abhartach? Who knows what horrors lie out there in the growing darkness of the Celtic night.

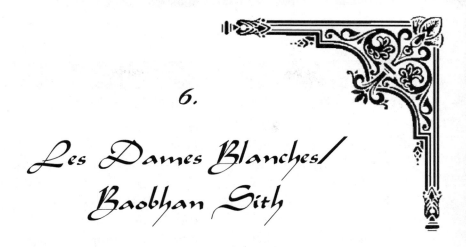

6.

Les Dames Blanches/ Baobhan Sith

FRANCE/SCOTLAND

omen have always played a central and important role in Celtic lore. They were the early goddesses, governing the births, lives, and deaths of individuals and controlling fertility and the crops, as well as the winds and weather—important attributes in agricultural communities. Celtic goddesses were also often war-like and the outcome of conflicts could sometimes depend upon their slightest whim. Mortal women were also supposed to have strange powers. For example, many of them were supposed to be able to foresee the future; although, in some parts of the Celtic world—in Scotland, for instance—the prognostications of a woman were considered to be less accurate than those of a man.

Women and the Supernatural World

There were two areas, however, in which there was a strong connection between women and the supernatural world. These were the areas of death and of the fairies. The image of the keening woman lying over the body of a fallen Celtic chieftain on the battlefield, or crouched, weeping, in the corner of some rural cottage is very well known in legend and artwork. Similarly, fairies seem to be attracted to women—particularly elderly women. It is not surprising, therefore, that these two elements have been drawn together in a number of folktales. Curiously, there is also a vampiric dimension to some of these tales.

Leanan Sidhe

Stories of blood-drinking fairies appear in the folklore of Ireland and the Western Isles of Scotland. *Glaistigs* (sometimes seen as malevolent and violent spirits) were said to inhabit ruined fortresses and abandoned churches in the Scottish West, terrifying and attacking passers-by. Here, too, are tales of men who have been lured away into mountain caves and bogs by the *Leanan Sidhe* (fairy lover/mistress), who then strangles them and either eats them or drinks their blood.

This horrid monster often takes the form of a beautiful woman whose mesmeric gaze no man can resist. Echoes of this creature are found right across the Celtic world from Brittany to the Isle of Man—the symbol of love and death. Such creatures have provided inspirations for writers, musicians, and poets whilst drawing out their life's energies and leaving them withered husks.

Midnight Washerwomen

It was a short leap of the imagination to see these creatures as the spirits of the dead who would waylay strangers with vampiric thoughts on their minds. In Brittany, they became the Midnight Washerwomen who, although not strictly vampiric, were still a danger to late-night travellers. A meeting with them would usually result in death. Waiting at crossroads (an evil place in the folklore of many cultures), these unfortunates are condemned to wash the funeral shrouds of those who are about to die or of unbaptized children.

Legend says that the Washerwomen are in fact the souls of those women who have committed some evil when alive or who have neglected their religious duties, and therefore are forced to wait at a point where roads cross for all eternity as a punishment. Those who pass them by are invited to help them fold the shrouds. The shroud-material is long, heavy, and unwieldy, and the folding takes the form of a kind of dance. If the traveller completes this successfully, he is allowed to pass on his way. However, if a mistake is made, then he is strangled by the Midnight Washerwomen in the shroud that they have been folding.

Such explanations have been used to account for bodies found along the sides of remote country roads (especially near crossings) that today we might ascribe to, say, sudden heart attacks.

Le Grand Bissetere

According to French folklore, another supernatural creature, *Le Grand Bissetere*, sometimes hovers around forest roads and woodland pools in rural Provence, making low moaning sounds, which would sometimes pass for the cry of a screech owl. To meet with this entity was considered extremely unlucky because it could draw the life from those whom it encountered and leave them for dead. Those who heard its eerie cry deep in the woods quickened their step and hurried on toward their destination.

Glaistig

In Scotland, too, strange cries echoed across the lonely lochs and deep, shadowy glens. This was the cry of the glaistig, an eerie being that often inhabited old ruins and, like the Leanan Sidhe, often took the form of a beautiful woman. And like her Irish counterpart, she used her good looks to lure male travellers from the path and into her clutches, where she drank their blood and drained off their energies. Their bodies were then discarded in the lochs, bogs, and rivers, which were often her home. The motif of the vampire-fairy was already well established in the Celtic mind.

Traits of les Dames Blanches

In a sense, the notion of *les Dames Blanches* was a combination of many of these folkloric elements. The name means "White Ladies" and usually referred to a type of creature that appeared to be half-ghost and half-fairy, but with definite vampiric tendencies. The name also suggests that there was usually more than one of them and that they travelled in groups. They were, for all intents and purposes, a variation of the Midnight Washerwomen, usually congregating around crossroads or cemeteries late at night and when the moon was full. Said to take the form of very beautiful women, their skin was as pale as ivory, and even on summer nights both their breath and touch were cold. Each night they would dance beneath the moon, inviting passers-by to join with them. No one refused, for the women were said to have hypnotic powers, which sapped any resistance to their call. Once in their freezing embrace, the hapless traveller was doomed. Drained of blood, his body would be found at the side of the road, where les Dames Blanches had thrown it.

The ladies were said to be the emanations of an ancient goddess: Druantia, Our Lady of the Oak. In Celtic mythology, she was believed to be the Queen of the Druids and the entity from which these Celtic wisemen received their powers. An ambivalent deity, she could either dispense well-being and healing through many of the herbs and fungi that grew in her woodlands; but she could also be dark and dangerous, as she

also presided over witchcraft and evil sorcery. In France, areas that had been strongholds of Druidic belief, les Dames Blanches were supernaturally linked to this darker side. She could give and preserve life, but she could also take it away—and she did this through her agents. French folklorists such as Anatole La Braz and F.M. Luzel regaled their readers and audiences with stories of the "night dancers at the crossroads"—sometimes portraying them as women, at other times as ugly dwarves, but always with malefic intent. The portraits that they paint are indeed eerie—pallid and beautifully gaunt women dancing in the moonlight without music (for there is no sound as les Dames Blanches dance) and beckoning travellers to their doom. Small wonder wayfarers did their best to avoid lonely roads and crossings.

Protection Against les Dames Blanches

There was little protection against the attentions of these creatures, and what protections there were often had to be offered by the Christian Church. A crucifix, for example, might turn them away, as would a blessing by a priest or cure, given to the traveller before the commencement of his or her journey. Similarly, calling on the Holy Name for aid was sometimes enough to make the Ladies disappear. There were, however, older, more pagan-based, protections, which suggested the great antiquity of the belief. A piece of iron carried somewhere on the person—in the pocket or in the hand, perhaps—would be sufficient to ward away the Ladies. Iron was, of course, an extremely ancient protective element and was used to dispel demons, ghosts, and spirits.

Baobhan Sith

Distantly related to les Dames Blanches was Scottish Baobhan Sith. Like her French counterparts, this creature enjoyed a pedigree that stretched back across many hundreds of years. The name meant "spirit woman," and the term *Sith* suggests a great antiquity, as it referred to the "people of the mounds," who were said to have occupied Scotland in the pagan times, long before the coming of Christianity. These were also the "fah-ri" (fairy) or "spirit people." The Baobhan Sith was usually a solitary spirit, often described as being somewhere between a ghost, a fairy, and a witch. In some areas she was considered a demon whose intentions were always malefic.

In Scottish folklore, throughout the 16th, 17th, and 18th centuries, the distinctions between fairies, witches, and demons were very blurred. In several Scottish witchcraft trials, such as that of Bessie Dunlop, who was strangled and burned in Ayrshire in 1576, fairies were closely associated with rural sorcerers. In return for succour, fairies supplied witches with their powers and knowledge, and aided them in their diabolic tasks. Consequently, fairies became little short of demons themselves. They set out to lead God's people astray or to kill them, both priests and ministers declared, sending their souls to the perdition of their master (satan). The Baobhan Sith was one of these dark and evil spirits.

Descriptions of her vary. In some instances, she closely resembles a member of les Dames Blanches but, unlike them, she did not necessarily haunt lonely crossroads. The being is invariably female and is often portrayed in Scottish folklore as a tall, pale woman with freezing cold skin and breath—an exact replica of her French counterpart. Her victims, however, are not lone wayfarers but the shepherds and herders who inhabit the isolated *sheilings* and *clachans* (huts and herders hamlets) of the Scottish hills and mountains. Mainly, she confined her attentions to the far Highlands and coastal West, but there are some accounts of her appearing in the East and in the Lowlands as well. In all the legends she is, like les Dames Blanches, vampiric, drinking the blood of sleeping men.

Although she appears as a tall woman in some Highland areas, there are other stories where she appears as a small, dark woman with a human upper body and the hindquarters and feet of a goat. The cloven hoof was, it is thought, an attempt by rural people to directly connect the Baobhan Sith with the Devil himself. In this incarnation, the being dwelt in the high mountains where the shepherds kept their sheep, coming out only in the late evening to stalk its victims through the glens and ravines. The Baobhan Sith would also appear to have had some control over the elements, creating the dank fogs that swept down out of nowhere across the mountains, enabling the creature to creep up on its victims unseen. Other stories tell how it was able to change its form and shape—chameleon-like—so that it appeared as a loved one or as somebody known to its victim. It then drew close to its victim, eventually springing at him like a wild animal and drawing his blood. At night, the entity would also turn up at the doors of remote mountain huts, where shepherds were lodging, in the guise of a loved one to be admitted and then pounce upon its prey.

In her book *The Supernatural Highlands*, Frances Thompson outlines one such tale that has at least some echoes of les Dames Blanches:

> Three men were hunting amongst the hills of Kintail. They had very little success but were reluctant to come away empty-handed. They therefore decided to try again the following day and that they would pass the night in a deserted hut high up in the hills. Settling themselves down, they lit a fire, cooked some venison and made themselves as comfortable as they could on some dry grass and moss. Two of them sat on one side of the fire whilst the third lay on the other, amongst the shadows, playing on a trump (a jew's harp). One of them passed an opinion that it was a long and lonely night, up here in the sheiling, and that he wished that his sweetheart was here with him—a sentiment with which the other heartily

agreed. Suddenly, there was a hammering on the door, which instantly opened to admit three women. By this time, the fire had burned low, casting a smoky, ruddy half-light through the shieling but even in the gloom the men were able to see the faces of the loved ones that they'd been longing for. The women sat down to warm themselves by the dying embers of the fire and the two nearest the heat turned to the men beside them. The other hunter—the one that had been playing the trump—sat back and watched as his companions embraced their sweethearts. But, it seemed to him, in the fading firelight, that the faces of the women shifted and moved and became the faces other females that he didn't know. Something wet touched the leg of his trousers and, looking down, he saw to his horror a stream of blood trickling across the floor of the hut from the other side of the embers. It was already forming in pools by the hearthstones around the edges of the fire. And in the dim light, he suddenly saw that the feet of the women who set opposite him were like those of a deer or goat (that is, cloven hoofed) and he realised with a chill that these were not mortal women at all but Baobhan Sith who were haunting these remote uplands. With a cry, he dropped the trump and fled from the hut, barely leaving the rough door on its hinges. With his lungs almost bursting from fear and effort, he dashed across the hill outside and, as he did so, the words of one of the creatures floated to him on the thin night air. "*Dhith sibhs'ur cuthauch fein ach dh'fhag mo cuthaich fein mise!*" ("You ate your own victims but mine escaped from me!") He ran, his lungs nearly bursting, until he reached the door of a human cottage where he collapsed on the floor and blurted out his story. In the morning, the bodies of his companions, drained of their blood and badly mangled, were found lying beside the ashes of their fire in the lonely sheiling. Many of the locals round about put their deaths down to the "fairy furies," as the Baobhan Sith are known in that area of Kintail. In other parts of the same area, they are known as "Highland Maenads" because of their wild and ferocious appearance when in their natural state.

In other parts of Scotland, the Baobhan Sith appears as a tall, gaunt, pale woman dancing in the moonlight, close to lochs, rivers, or bogs. Indeed, the creature seems to have an affinity for water and will often invite shepherds who are seeking their sheep to dance with it before dragging them into the loch or bog and draining them of their blood. In some regions of the Highlands, it is portrayed almost as a skeleton, dressed in long, flowing robes with long, pointed, vampire teeth, dancing alone in the shadows under the trees or on the empty moor, waiting for someone to pass by. For this reason, Scottish herders and shepherds tended to avoid isolated standing stones and lonely moorland crosses (which were closely associated with this being) or gloomy hollows in which the Baobhan Sith might be lurking.

As with les Dames Blanches, it is advisable to carry a piece of iron—preferably an iron nail that has never shod a horse—about one's person as a form of protection against the being's advances. A holy medal or scapular would also offer protection, and this fact led some Scottish Lowland Presbyterian reformers to declare that the Baobhan Sith were only associated with Catholics living in the Highlands. They believed that a strong Presbyterian faith was as good a protection as any against the Devil and his agents.

An ancient folktale from South Uist in the Western Isles tells of a man looking for his goats on the North End of the Island.

In the shadow of a high cliff, he saw what he thought was a light or the glow of a fire and, imagining that it was one of his neighbors who was camping there, he made his way toward it. It was a bright moonlit night and the silvery strands of light fell from the clouds onto a tiny loch—little more than a pond—some way below. As the shepherd neared the light, he saw that it was some kind of lantern placed on a large rock, and that a figure came and went in front of it. It was a woman dancing in the gloom under the cliff—the shepherd looked at her moving shadow in amazement. As his eyes became more accustomed to the murk, he saw that she was very tall and also very beautiful. Seeing him standing there, she beckoned to him to come forward and join in her dance, and, almost against his will, he stepped forward. The woman moved in front of him again, and in a ray of moonlight he saw, not a beautiful lady, but a skeleton-like creature whose face was a glistening skull, with long and pointed fangs. It wore a long and tattered gown through which mildewed bones poked. In horror, he realized that this was a Baobhan Sith, and that it was drawing him into that lonely place in order to drink his blood. Being a good Catholic, he crossed himself and called upon the Name of the Virgin whereupon the light went out and the creature vanished, leaving only a faint reek of sulphur behind it—a hint of the creature's links with the Infernal Regions. The shepherd immediately fell to his knees and gave thanks for his miraculous escape and, as soon as he returned to his village, he went straight away to see his priest in case some taint of the vampire still clung to him.

The origins of les Dames Blanches and the Baobhan Sith are very ancient. But what are they? The returning dead; the last vestiges of an ancient goddess; the survivors of some long-lost, goat-footed, blood-drinking race that lived in the West long before the coming of the Celts? (There are many old tales of such a race—for example, the extremely ancient tale of King Herla, a Saxon ruler who met with one of their kings in the Dark Ages). Are they fairies? Maybe they are a combination of all of these. Maybe *something*—some vampiric entity—from the earliest times still lingers somewhere in the depths of the Western mind, changing and adapting as it passes down through the centuries—maybe *that* is the true legend of les Dames Blanches and the Baobhan Sith. But who can say?

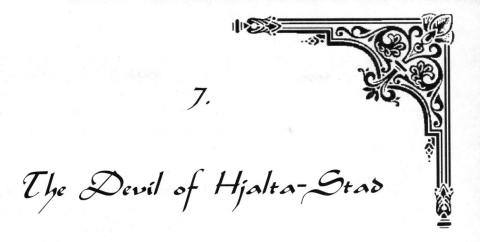

7.

The Devil of Hjalta-Stad

ICELAND

n Scandinavia, the nights are long, dark, and thought to be full of unnatural spirits and creatures. For the Norsemen, who lived in these cold climates in past centuries, ghosts and walking dead prowled the woods and wastes between the isolated settlements, intent on doing what harm to the living that they could.

Much of what we know about the Northern night-stalking dead comes from ancient Icelandic tales written by monks who were descendants of Norwegians who had colonized the inhospitable landscape centuries earlier. Many of the tales were written from a Christian perspective because, by the time of writing, much of Scandinavia had been converted to Christianity, a warning against the remnants of ancient pagan beliefs that still persisted. These were tales of the uncoffined corporeal dead who lay in their burial mounds, scattered all through

the land recorded in sagas that were handed down in the monastic libraries. Amongst these were types of stories known as *eventyr* or *aeventyr* stories of strange occurrences or supernatural happenings. Amongst these were tales of the returning dead.

The early Vikings had believed that the spirits (and sometimes the actual bodies) of those who died in battle went straight to Valhalla, the endless Hall of Heroes, a kind of warrior's heaven where the dead feasted, caroused, and fought. What happened to those who did not die in conflict was much more problematic. Possibly their spirits and their bodies lay in some form of limbo—not quite left this world but not quite alive either. Even so, many of these dead behaved as if they *were* still alive. They ate, they drank, they could copulate and, because they were corporeal, they could exact revenge on their former enemies. Rising from their tomb-mounds, eerie revenants sometimes prowled the edges of villages, carrying swords or axes and seeking out those whom they believed had done them wrong—just as they would have done in life. Under cover of darkness, they would then enter the settlements and take their revenge, usually murdering those whom they sought.

The Draugr

Such beliefs led to a general unease amongst the living concerning the dead. Those living close to mounds or tombs where dead warriors lay were often nervous about their unsettled "neighbors." They referred to them as *draugr*, or marauders, who might attack them at any time. Another name, *aptrgangr* (literally, "one who walks after death") signaled an entity that was just as frightening and vicious. The term simply became a generalized description for the malevolent wandering dead. Draugr were easily recognized because of their skin coloring. This could either be *hel-blar* (death blue) or *na-foir* (corpse pale). There was also the unmistakable reek of decay

and corruption about it. What was so frightening about these hostile creatures was that they had immense strength and could increase the size of their bodies at will. In some ancient tales, the bodies of the walking dead had almost doubled or tripled in size, perhaps due to gasses or the drinking of fresh blood. These draugr killed their opponents simply by crushing them, and then they either devoured the flesh or drank the blood of their victims. In such cases, the victim was likely to become a draugr himself. The only way to defeat one of these things was to wrestle with it, defeat it, and return it to its tomb, for it couldn't really be destroyed except possibly by fire and it was believed that these beings were virtually unstoppable. In the "Eyrbyggi Saga," a shepherd is beset by a draugr, which is of black-blue coloring, and has his neck broken by the force of its grip—he later returns as one of the Undead himself.

The Haugbui

In later years, the idea of the walking dead became slightly more specific. In addition to the draugr, there were also the *haugbui* (barrow dwellers or "sleepers in the mounds"). These might be just as ferocious as the draugr, but they only attacked those who trespassed on the area where they lay. Scandinavian burial practices varied; there were ship-burials and cairn burials, as well as several forms of cremation and internment in Christian gravesites. The most common form of burial, however, was in the barrow. This was a purpose-built stone chamber, roofed with wood and covered with thick clods of earth, so that it resembled a grassy mound. Such mounds were usually near a family dwelling and were often tended by family members. Traditionally, a person had to be able to name all his ancestors who had previously held the land and to name those who lay in a particular barrow before he could formally inherit the land. Not to be able to do so was considered an insult to the "honored dead." It was also considered that such mounds were also the resting places of great treasures and costly items, and references to these are to be found in many of the sagas.

In the Norse mind, the ideas of the dead and hidden treasures were also linked with beliefs about dwarves and trolls— hardy and often irascible creatures that were said to live under the ground. In his translation of *The Poetic Edda* (1962), Lee M. Hollander tells us that the names of "deep dwelling dwarves" in *Dvergatal* ("Catalogue of Dwarves") are suggestive of cold, desolation, and death. (Incidentally, it is interesting to note that one of the names used in this ancient work—Gandalf— was later used as the name of a powerful wizard by J.R.R. Tolkein in his epic *Lord of the Rings*.) The dwarves guarded their treasures and so did the Undead. Although some personal wealth was undoubtedly secreted in the tombs of ancestors, it was a brave grave robber who would try to take it. The haugbui jealously guarded the valuables that lay in the grave

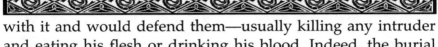

with it and would defend them—usually killing any intruder and eating his flesh or drinking his blood. Indeed, the burial mound came to be regarded as the haugbui's house, and any interloper was regarded as a marked man.

The sleepers in the mound could sometimes be rather unpredictable as well. From time to time they could leave their tombs and attack those who lived nearby their "houses" or passers-by for no apparent reason. The "Eyrbyggia Saga," for example recounts the tale of Thorolf Halt-foot, a man of ill temper when alive and worse when he returned as a draugr, marauding and killing in the countryside round about his tomb at certain times of the year. He seems to have travelled through the surrounding countryside, accompanied by several other Undead companions in a kind of expedition reminiscent of the Wild Hunt, destroying property and killing shepherds and herders. No one could stand up to him, for the only way to destroy a draugr of this sort was to wrestle it to defeat. He was finally constrained by building a stone wall around his tomb. Even then, Thorolf proved difficult to restrain and, following several deaths in the locality, it was realized that he was wandering about once more. Consequently, his body was dug up and burnt. The corpse was placed on a pyre and the wind was allowed to blow over the remains of the fire, scattering the ashes all over the landscape. The Saga continues, telling how a cow, after licking the stones on which Thorolf's ashes had settled, later gave birth to a monstrous bull that caused more death and mayhem round about. The violent spirit of Thorolf Halt-foot had not gone away.

Although draugr and haugbui appeared physically solid and could both strangle an individual or deliver substantial blows to his or her body, they could also rise or disappear through the ground, like smoke. This was, no doubt, effective in attacking those who were crossing over, or who passed too close to their tombs: the draugr could suddenly rise from the earth and then sink back into it at will. It was therefore wise to

stay away from such places. In the case of Thorolf Halt-foot, any animal that grazed close to his tomb howled piteously or went mad. And in some other instances, cattle, horses, and even dogs were found dead and drained of blood close to the barrow. Great lumps of raw flesh had also been torn from some of the animals' sides in order to feed the draugr's hunger. Sometimes, the creature would even attack shepherds and herders. In some cases, those looking after sheep near upland graves never returned home.

Protection Against the Draugr

There was little protection against the things and often what protections there were could be associated with black magic. Witness the case of the unfortunate Sigurdur Jonsson, who was burnt as a witch at Pingvellir, Iceland, in 1671. Faced with a hostile draugr, he drove it away with a mixture of herbs and his own semen. This, to the authorities in the county of Isafjardarsyslla, suggested a knowledge of things far beyond ordinary men, and so the unfortunate Sigurdur was brought to trail, found guilty, and executed. Even the most peripheral dealings with the Viking Undead could have fatal consequences.

Because the draugr and haugbui were difficult to defeat, argued the wise, prevention was far better than any cure. The walking dead had to be stopped from rising or from entering a house and killing the inhabitants in order to drink their blood or eat their flesh. Therefore, even in Christian Scandinavia, old and established pagan practices were often conducted at funerals. A pair of open iron scissors were often laid on the chest of a corpse, whilst small pieces of straw or twigs might be laid under the shroud or concealed amongst the clothing. The great toes might also be tied together so that the legs could not be separated and therefore the cadaver could not walk. Needles might also be run into the soles of the feet for exactly the same purpose, and, when the coffin was being carried out of the house, the bearers were required to raise it and lower it three times and in three different directions (usually in the form of a cross) to confuse the "sleeper" within. When the coffin had left the house, the chairs on which it had rested (and indeed sometimes all chairs) were overturned and all jars and bottles turned upside down. Certain incantations might be offered up at the graveside as the coffin was being lowered to hold the occupant fast.

The most effective means of preventing the returning Undead, said tradition, was the "corpse door." Although this belief may have originated in Denmark, it soon spread across the entire Norse world. A special door was added to a building, through which the corpse was carried, feet-first, and then the entrance was bricked up again so that it would not return. It was widely believed that the walking dead could only enter a building by the way in which they had left it, and so this was denied them. As the coffin left the house, mourners clustered around it to prevent the corpse from having a clear view as to where it was going.

As Christianity established itself throughout Scandinavia, the notion of vengeful revenants became linked with notions of black magic and sorcery. The dead had always been associated with witchcraft and shamanism in the Northern mind, but now it took on a much more formal tone. It was believed, for instance, that parts of a dead human body might be used in awful and hideous spells. The *nabrok trousers*, for example, sometimes worn by black magicians, consisted of the lower portions of a dead man's torso that had been flayed from one who had been executed for some crime (if the crime was murder, so much the better). When these were worn by a magician, gold would collect in the scrotum, or so tradition said. However, only those with the blackest souls might wear such ghastly breeches. In 1656, Jon Jonsson Jr. was burnt at Isafjordur during the Icelandic witchcraft trials, for using powdered human

remains in the preparation of *fretrunir* (farting runes), which he then used against a local girl whom he disliked and to cause the sickness of the Reverend Jon Magnusson. It was further said that somewhere in Iceland was the famous Black School, which used cadavers to teach magicians abominable magics. The dead and dark sorcery were therefore closely linked in the Nordic mind.

Black Magicians

It was a small leap from this concept to the notion that the malicious dead could either be raised or controlled by black magicians. This power, it was thought, could be exercised by powerful wizards—some of whom were possibly churchmen! One of the most notorious of these magicians was Bishop Gottskelk the Evil of Holar (1497–1520), who was said to have compiled a grimoire of ghastly magic—the Raudeskein (Red-Skin Cover)—that contained numerous spells for the raising of the dead and for directing them against the living. Many of these involved designs for the making of magic "staves" (though whether these were actually carved wooden staffs or simply runic drawings is not wholly clear). The most famous and most powerful of these "staves" was the Aeishjalmur, the "helm of awe," which was able to turn recently buried corpses into draugr that would attack the living and drink their blood and devour their flesh. These animated bodies, said conventional wisdom, contained devils that the magician had summoned from the very pit of hell.

Thus, dark, vampiric cadavers prowled the Nordic countryside (particularly in Iceland, where, it was once thought, witches and sorcerers abounded), entering houses and killing the inhabitants at the behest of malicious wizards and evil churchmen. Some were said to be controlled by masters from the infamous Black School, which was said to lie amongst the frozen wastes of Northern Iceland. Many of these ghouls

engaged in what might be today termed as antisocial behavior, which made them even more feared.

And there was more. It was believed in many parts of the Nordic world that black magicians could cause harm to those whom they disliked by a process known as *mundklemm*, or *mundklem* (the spellings vary)—the stealing of the breath. The result of this process was invariably fatal for the victim, whose vital energies were "drawn off" by the sorcerer, mostly operating at a distance, until the body became totally exhausted and the heart stopped.

Witches, often in the guise of cats or voles, scurried about the countryside, seeking to wreak this evil against their neighbors. Today we would probably diagnose this as some form of heart condition, but, for the early Norse, it was most assuredly witchcraft. If witches could perform such a spell, it was argued, so could the walking dead—who, after all, might actually be controlled by black magicians. Thus, a cadaver might lurk near a homestead, drawing away the "good" of the house or creating disease there. From time to time, they might even venture into the building, killing those within, eating their flesh and drinking their blood.

The Devil of Hjalta-Stad

The most famous of all these walking, blood-drinking dead was widely known as the Devil of Hjalta-Stad. Mention of the creature first appears in a letter to Bishop Haldorr Brynjolfsson, written by Sheriff Hans Wium in the autumn of 1750. The drugr was said to have been in the form of a bald old man, wrapped in ragged grave-clothes, prowling the ancient burial ground at Hjalta-Stad, as well as a house nearby. Although nothing is known about the exact origins of this spectre, it was thought to have been the phantom of an old man with an evil and disagreeable temperament, long suspected of being a witch. The thing attacked people passing by the

cemetery, often causing them physical injury and spilling their blood. It also threw stones and called obscenities at terrified onlookers, threatening them in the most appalling manner.

Under the Nordic law of the time, the secular authorities could become involved in this matter; hence, the sheriff's interest in the case. It was thought that the secular authorities could compel a cadaver to answer a summons and give an account of itself before an officer of the law though, understandably, such summonses were seldom invoked. However, Sheriff Wium seems to have taken a particular interest in the phantom, and his letter gives us an insight into 18th century Icelandic views of the night-walking (and often vampiric) dead. He writes:

> The Devil at Hjalta-Stad was outspoken enough this past winter, although no one saw him. I, along with others had the dishonour to hear him talking for nearly two days, during which he addressed myself and the minister, Sir Grim, with words the like of which 'eye hath not seen nor ear heard'. As soon as we reached the front of the house there was heard in the door an iron voice saying:'So Hans from Eyrar is come now, and wishes to talk with me, the idiot'. Compared with other names that he gave me this might be considered as flattering. When I inquired who it was that addressed me with such words, he answered in a fierce voice,"I was called Lucifer at first, but now I am called Devil and Enemy" He threw at us both stones and pieces of wood, as well as other things, and broke two windows in the minister's room. He spoke so close to us that he seemed to be just at our side. There was an old woman there of the name of Opia whom he called his wife, and a 'heavenly blessed soul' and asked Sir Grim to marry them, with various other remarks of this kind, which I will not recount.
>
> I have little liking to write about his outgoings, which were all disgraceful and shameful in accordance with the nature of the actor. He repeated the 'Pater Noster' three times, answered

questions from the Catechism and the Bible, said that the devils hold service in hell, and told what texts and psalms they had for various occasions. He asked us to give him some of the food we had, and a drink of tea etc. I asked the fellow whether God was good. He said 'Yes'. Whether he was truthful. He answered, 'Not one of his words can be doubted' Sir Grim asked him whether the devil was good-looking. He answered; 'He is far better looking than you, you ugly snout!' I asked him whether the devils agreed well with each other. He answered in a kind of sobbing voice: 'It is painful to know that they never have peace'. I bade him say something to me in German, and said to him '*Lass uns Teusc redre* (sic), but he answered as if he had misunderstood me.

When we went to bed in the evening, he shouted fiercely, in the middle of the floor. 'On this night I shall snatch you off to hell, and you shall not rise up out of the bed as you lay down'. During the evening, he wished the minister's wife good-night. The minister and I continued to talk with him during the nigh, among other things we asked him what kind of weather it was outside. He answered: 'It is cold, with a north wind'. We asked if he was cold. He answered: 'I think I am both hot and cold'. I asked him how loud he could shout. He said, 'So loud that the roof would go off the house and you would all fall into a dead faint'. I told him to try it. He answered: 'Do you think I an come here to amuse you, you idiot?' I asked him to show us a little specimen. He said he would do so, and gave three shouts, the last of which was so fearful that I have never heard anything worse, and doubt whether I ever shall. Towards daybreak, after he had parted from us with the usual compliments, we fell asleep.

Next morning, he came in again, and began to waken up people, he named each one by name, not forgetting to name some nickname, and asking whether so-and so was awake. When he saw they were all awake, he said he was going to play with the door now, and with that he threw the door of its

hinges with a sudden jerk, and sent it far in upon the floor. The strangest thing was that when he threw anything it went down at once, and then went back to its place again, so it was evident that he either went inside it or moved about with it.

The previous evening he challenged me twice to come out into the darkness to him, and this is an angry voice, saying that he would tear me limb from limb. I went out and told him to come on, but nothing happened. When I went back to my place and asked him why he had not fulfilled his promise, he said: 'I had no orders for it from my master'. (John Arnason, *Icelandic Folklore and Fairy* Tales, *vol.* i., p. 309)

Another narrative of 1808 states:

[The Devil] asked us whether we had ever heard the like before, and when we said 'Yes', he answered. 'That is not true, the like has never been heard at any time'. He had sung 'The memory of Jesus' after I arrived there, and talked frequently while the word of God was being read. He said that he did not mind this, but that he did not like the 'Cross School Psalms' and said it must have been a great idiot who composed them. This enemy came like a devil and departed as such, and behaved himself as such while he was present, nor would it benefit anyone but the devil to declare all that he said. At the same time it must be added that I am not quite convinced that it was a spirit, but my opinions on this I cannot give here for lack of time.

Apparently, several attempts were made in order to explain at least part of the phenomenon away. Some recorded variations of the sheriff's letter attribute the peculiar voice to a young local man who had learned ventriloquism whilst travelling abroad. Yet, the sheriff himself dismisses such explanations,

stating that no human voice could have produced the terrifying roars of the Devil or whether a number of personal questions, which were asked, could have been answered correctly, as was the case.

When the Devil of Hjalta-Stad finally disappeared is unknown. John Arnason's *Icelandic Folklore and Fairy Tales* makes mention of it and refers to the sheriff's letter, but makes no further mention of the haunting, whilst the more sceptical writer Jon Espolin, in his *Annals*, tries to discredit the whole episode and declares that the Devil never existed at all and that the story is just a fable thought up by uncouth minds.

So what is the truth of the tale? Was it all a hoax or was the corpse of an evil old man indeed animated by the Devil in 17th-century Iceland? Whatever the facts of the matter, the Devil of Hjalta-Stat serves as a fine example of a Norse draugr—that malignant, often vampiric being that lurked out in the growing gloom as the northern night descended, lurking there with a dark and evil intent.

8.

The Dybbuk

HEBREW

In some cultures the distinction between vampire and demon is rather blurred. It should not be assumed that demons are always evil or wholly malignant, though in Christian tradition they invariably are. The word *demon* comes from the Greek word for "spirit," which is sometimes translated as "inspiration, Muse, or motivating force." Consequently, in some cases, demons could be ambivalent in nature, spurring individuals toward acts of creativity as well as acts of great wickedness. The vampiric demon known as the dybbuk (also known as the *gilgul* or "clinging soul") manifests elements of this ambivalence within Hebrew folklore.

Semitic Folklore

Forms of vampirism were not unusual amongst the early Semites. It was believed, for example, amongst the early Hebrews (and amongst some other ancient peoples as well) that certain people could magically draw both strength and vitality from others simply by being near to them or by touching them. Aged men or women who were frail and feeble would sometimes seek out youngsters to sit or lie with them in order to draw off their energies by a kind of osmotic process. If an old man lay with a young woman, it was argued, he could "draw off" some of her youth into himself in vampire fashion.

So prevalent was this belief amongst the Semites that it has found its way into the Bible. The King James version carefully censors it, but a thinly veiled reference to the practice appears in a tale concerning the elderly King David, recounted in 1 Kings 1–4:

> *Now King David was old and stricken in years and they covered him with clothes but he gat (sic) no heat. Wherefore his servants said unto him, Let there be sought for my lord the king, a young virgin and let her stand before the king and let her cherish him and let her lie in thy bosom, that my lord the king may get heat. So they sought for a fair damsel throughout all the coasts of Israel and found Abishag a Shummanite and brought her to the king. And the damsel was very fair and cherished the king and ministered to him but the king knew her not.*

Hidden in this formal biblical reference are hints of very early Semitic magic and folklore. Perhaps the more sanitized King James version has glossed over them, but traces of folklore are still there. The frail and elderly king is long past his best and seeks something to restore his vigor, enabling him to continue to rule. His servants suggest that he lie with a young girl in order to "absorb" her vitality into himself,

allowing him to deal with threatened revolts, which are consuming the country. And so Abishag is brought to him and lies with him ("cherishes him," as the King James's quaintly puts it) in order to restore his vitality. The union is not a sexual one—the text is very specific on that ("the king knew her not")—but is simply one of a magical energy-transference. Some Middle Eastern traditions also held that certain *kahins* (early Arabian oracle-mongers) could draw the life force from their victims even over a distance. (Interestingly, this belief was also held by the Vikings from Scandinavia who thought that Norse witches—particularly those in Orkney and the Northern Isles—could actually draw the life from those whom they disliked, even over a distance of many miles. The process or spell was known as *Mundklem* or "the stealing of the breath.") In the later Jewish tradition, some rabbis were thought to have the power to draw the energies from dissident members of their congregations as a means of punishment or admonition.

If certain of the living might have the ability to absorb the vitality of those around them, then the dead also enjoyed such powers. And the souls of the dead were everywhere. Although the bodies were turned to dust, the spirits lingered on for various reasons and became known as *gilgul*, strictly speaking, souls in a state of transmigration from this world to the Afterlife. Because these spirits often refused to leave the world of the living, they were sometimes referred to as "clinging souls." Later they came to be known as *dybbuk*. Not only could these spirits—in effect, ghosts—draw away a person's vitality by invisibly swarming through the air and around him or her, but they could also *occupy the physical body*, drawing sustenance from within like a parasite. This partly laid the foundation for the notion of spirit/demon possession, which was to concern the early Christian Church (Christianity, of course, had its roots in Judaism). And like the early Christian demons, the dybbuk could enter the body

through any orifice, particularly the mouth and nose. Writing of Christian demons, Pope Gregory the Great mentions a nun who became possessed by eating a cabbage leaf upon which a demon was invisibly perched. She had not, said the pontiff, made the sign of the cross, and so the demon gained control of her. Because the dybbuk, or clinging souls, swarmed everywhere, they could settle on food or be consumed in drink, and they could also be ingested by breathing impure air or fumes. A legendary eighth-century Middle-Eastern scroll, referred to as *The Testament of the Patriarchs*, sometimes rendered as *Tales of the Kahins*, is believed to counsel against entering miniature dust storms or whirlwinds, or going into caves or ruined buildings that have been closed up for some time, as this is where such spirits dwell and thrive.

However, the description and attributes of the dybbuk are vague and confused, and seem to be more appropriate to the *Sheddim*—hairy, unclean, goat-like demons that dwell in the wilderness. No clear definition of the clinging soul seems to exist much before rabbinical lore the 15th and 16th centuries. Like their Christian counterparts, the rabbis were concerned about attack and possession by supernatural forces and sought to find ways to avoid it. This concern reached a peak in the rabbinical school of Isaac Luria (1534–1572) and in the writings of his chief disciple, Chayim Vital, and it is here that a clear notion of a dybbuk as a distinct and malefic entity first really begins to appear. But, even before then, rabbis were aware of strength-sapping entities entering the bodies of the faithful. Medieval Jewish literature, especially the works on *Hasidei Askhenaz*, is filled with detailed and practical advice on avoiding and placating demons and "wandering souls."

Traits of the Dybbuk

When the dybbuk entered the body, certain changes were clearly observed. The person so possessed became tired and

listless, and began to fail; he or she began to twitch or some-times vomit a whitish foam; and might act out of character. Rabbis drew attention to the dark entity that overtook King Saul of Israel (1 Samuel 16: 1–4) and caused the king to fly into a wild and inexplicable rage. Saul was himself guilty of draw-ing down spirits when he had the Witch of Endor ("a pytho-ness") summon the spirit of Samuel so that he could question it. The Talmud further states that, in order to help Rabbi Shimmon bar Yochai have anti-Jewish decrees annulled, a spirit, or dybbuk, entered the body of the emperor's daugh-ter, causing her to turn pale and foam at the mouth. However, upon Rabbi Shimmon's command, it departed and the girl was returned to full health.

It is not surprising, then, that these entities were believed to spread death and disease—a feature of vampires in other countries as well. Local communities strongly associated them with plague and wasting illnesses, and even the slight-est sickness might be attributed to the visit of a vampire in some parts of the world. Dybbuk were also associated with such diseases as epilepsy and swooning fits because it was considered that at the time of the fit, the creature fed, debili-tating its host almost to the point of unconsciousness. The vampiric dybbuk, it was argued, fed on the strength of its host, causing him or her to waste away and eventually die. Food was of no use to the sufferer because the dybbuk drew the "goodness" from its victim into itself in order to perpetu-ate its own awful existence.

When writing of the dybbuk, the Sephardic Jews, particu-larly those who had studied the Kabbalah, or works of Jewish mysticism, distinguished between two differing types of su-pernatural beings. One was the "clinging soul"—the wander-ing soul of a person already dead, which, for various reasons, had still not left the living world and had taken up its habitation in the body of a still-living person. The other was an entity that had never truly lived but was just as malignant and

dangerous. The *Testament of the Patriarchs* (thought to have been written in the second century B.C., and which outlines lives and lore of heroes from the Old Testament) seems to suggest that these were either the children of Lilith (the first wife of Adam who had given birth to more than 1,000 demons and supernatural beings later known as *Liln*) or something created by sorcery. The Testament seems to suggest that certain early Semitic magicians could create powerful and malevolent creatures using dust and menstrual blood (it was considered that blood issued during a woman's "unclean time"—when she was cursed by God—was incredibly potent in dark Jewish magic).

There may even have been a third type distinguished by the rabbis themselves: the *Yezer Ha-Ra*, a vampire-demon that lunged upon the dutiful worshipper as he or she left the Synagogue on a Friday night. This demon drained the vitality from its victim whilst at the same time filling his or her head with lustful thoughts of a terrible intensity. Different rites and rituals of expulsion were given for each type of dybbuk, and these could only be performed by a rabbi. As from the 17th century onward, the dybbuk had become a very complex entity, especially in parts of Europe where many Jews had settled.

Coupled with the sickness came an ability to prophecy—another unfailing sign that a dybbuk had taken over a person. Because the dead or supernatural entities could see the future, they could issue warnings and cautions. For example, Rabbi Vital tells of a young woman who was possessed of such a creature that made her waste away but also proclaimed itself as the spirit of an ancient sage who had lived in the Garden of Eden and had been sent by God with a special message. This, the dybbuk proclaimed, was to warn Rabbi Vital that the Damascan Jews were in extreme danger if they did not repent their sins. On hearing the message, the rabbi dismissed the dybbuk and it fled back from whence it came, and the girl began to recover immediately.

Becoming a Dybbuk

How did the spirit of a Jew become a clinging soul—a dybbuk? The answers were many and varied. There were, however, two main causes: if someone had died with a sin for which he or she had not formally atoned or if the person had not been buried in accordance with proper Jewish sacrament and ritual. An individual whom a rabbi had cursed, who had lived a dissolute life, or who had either deliberately or inadvertently broken Jewish dietary laws (for example, eating pork or mixing meat and dairy products) was also at risk. Suicides were almost certainly destined to become dybbuk. Other minor occurrences such as speaking harshly or not washing properly during life might also turn a dead soul into a dybbuk. Once it had become such a creature, the soul was always seeking to find a way back into the world or to sustain itself through the energies of those whom it encountered.

Protection Against a Dybbuk

How could a clinging soul be expelled? Because the entity itself was such a complicated being, the rites and rituals involved in dismissing it were also intricate and complex. They could only be performed by a rabbi and, moreover, a rabbi who had been given special training in exorcism. Fragments of rabbinical works on exorcism from all centuries can be found scattered all across Europe and the Middle East including Turino 1672 (*Egeret Ramaz*), Nicholsberg 1696 (Mosche ben Meanachem's *Sera HaKodesh*), and Jerusalem 1904 (S.R. Mizrachi's *Ma'aseh haruach shel Norah*).

Part of the most common formula used involved addressing the dybbuk directly and determining its identity (that is, its given name during its earthly life) bearing in mind that the entity, knowing full well what the rabbi is about, will seek to deliberately mislead him. This name can then be used

in certain invocations to expel the dybbuk. According to some exorcisms, a parchment, bearing certain sacred names written in a specific order must be hung around the victim's neck. Certain banishments rely on a mixture of Jewish and non-Jewish elements—the burning of sulphur; chants in both Hebrew and Latin; the inhaling of the smoke of certain sacred herbs.

But the rabbis all agreed on the principle that prevention was far better than cure, and that men and women had to be circumspect in their day-to-day observances to avoid having dybbuk enter their bodies. Circumcision was an especially dangerous time, and red ribbons and garlic had to be placed around a baby boy's crib prior to the act to ward off the malevolent entities. A piece of candy might also be placed near the infant because it was believed that the clinging souls (who sometimes came in the guise of flies) had a sweet tooth and might be distracted. In Eastern Europe, candy was replaced by raisins, sugared almonds, and pieces of cake to lure the vampires away from the infant. At certain times, glass might be broken close by because it was believed that the sound might frighten the dybbuk away (this was also carried out at weddings and was said to ensure the happiness of the bride and groom). Candles might also be lit close to young people, as the dybbuk were said to dislike the light and smoke.

Certain amulets might also be worn or hung from the doorpost or from the fringes of the *tefillin* (prayer shawl) as safeguards against dybbuk. They could be made of either wax or iron (though, understandably, the most effective were those made from metal). Some of them were inscribed with various letters of the different names of God or pictures of the Star of David, the *menonorah* (branched candle-stand or light), and an outstretched hand. Some invocations might also be used; for example, "My mother has told me to beware of shabriri, shabiri, biri, riri, iri, ri." (It is interesting to note that *shabiri* is the Hebrew word for "blindness" or "dim sight," which was a condition sometimes associated with attacks by dybbuk or

other demons.) There were further incantations, which might be used against the wasting of muscles or indeed a general languor, that were thought to be symptoms of dybbuk activity.

In some Jewish folktales, the dybbuk was said to dwell in specific parts of the human body—specifically the little finger or in one of the toes—and it was this that the rabbi addressed when seeking to expel the entity. Prior to the excommunication, a hole had to be drilled somewhere in a building to allow the creature, usually in the shape of a fly or moth, to escape. These holes were often made in window frames, and, if this was not done, the vampiric dybbuk would not leave the house but would attach itself to some other member of the family.

Dybbuk Folklore

From the 17th century onward, the dybbuk, as a clinging soul, possessing individuals and feeding upon their energies to sustain itself, became a part of Jewish folklore, particularly in Europe. As folktales about the entities began to proliferate, some of them found their way into forms of literary expression. S. Ansky (1863–1920), a Yiddish author and folklorist of the early 20th century, wrote one of the most celebrated dybbuk plays—*Der Dybbuk*—later translated into Hebrew by Chayim Nachman Bialik. This was performed by the Israeli acting troupe Habimah in Moscow, Tel-Aviv, and New York, and, in 1938, was turned into a film by a Polish-Yiddish production company.

An old book, *The Meysach Book* (*Book of Tales*), a collection of folk stories written around 1602, recounts the following tale:

> A young man was possessed by the wandering spirit (gilgul) of a dead man who had drowned at sea. The man's spirit had first of all passed into a cow; the cow had gone wild and the owner had sold it to a Jew; the Jew was about to slaughter the cow just as the young man passed by and the

spirit flew into the young man 's [sic] body. Once it had settled in its new home, it took over the young man 's [sic] mind, will and body. The young man had become its puppet. He began to waste away as the spirit settled into his body and could not even think for himself. Wise men came to help him. They asked *'Who are you?'* and the *dybbuk* spoke. He said that he was drowned at sea but, as his body had never been recovered, his wife was not permitted to re-marry and had eventually become a prostitute. These events made him extremely unhappy and, he revealed, he also bore the guilt of having committed adultery when alive. He was also able to see into the hearts of those around him and named certain sins that they themselves had committed and drawing further confessions from them. He thus acted as an agent for setting right ancient wrongs. He would have stayed in the body of the young man but his presence there was injurious to his host—making him weak, drawing the good out of him and threatening him with disease and death. He was finally persuaded to depart but to where is not known.

Even though many Western thinkers have tried to establish a link between the Hebrew dybbuk and Christian demons, the two are not exactly the same. The linking notion is of course that of spirit-possession because both types of being seek to possess individuals for their own purposes. However, whereas the demon/devil of Christian mythology is invariably portrayed as a wholly evil creature, the dybbuk is a much more ambivalent entity. When it draws energies from its host, in a vampire fashion, it usually does so simply in order to survive and not really for any wholly malefic reason.

There have been attempts also to link the dybbuk with another figure in Jewish folklore: the golem. Several Jewish folktales describe a creature made of clay that was created in medieval Prague by the Great Rabbi Yehudd Leow and that

took vengeance on the enemies of Judaism in that city. Some rabbinical traditions have claimed that the golem itself (the name simply means "raw and formless material") was motivated by a dybbuk, although it is usually agreed that Rabbi Leow created the creature himself out of dust, using the *Sefer Ha Yetzera* (*Book of Formation*) and one of the Kabbalistic secret names of God which was used to create man. Nevertheless, such attempts serve to show the centrality of the dybukk belief in general Jewish folklore.

The dybbuk, then, remains a complex and contradictory entity. It might well be counted as a vampire because it draws energies from the host that it occupies, causing them to waste away—and yet it is much more. Is it a demon? A ghost? A supernatural parasite? Who can say? The answer may lie somewhere amongst the mysteries of ancient Jewish superstition.

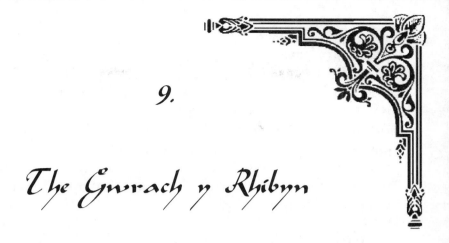

9.

The Gwrach y Rhibyn

WALES

Throughout Celtic mythology, the image of the hag, or old woman, has been a persistent one. Perhaps there is an element in the Celtic mind that looks back toward a mother-goddess from which all men (and indeed all creation) sprang. Early representations of an early grotesque female figure known as a Sile (or Sheelagh) na Gig—a creature with wasted breasts, a pot belly, a terrible face, and an extended vulva—are to be found across Ireland and were once more or less outlawed by the Church as symbols of paganism. Curiously, many of them appear in church doorways and niches, or the gates of abbeys, although this is probably to take away the inherent evil influence that was believed to attend them. In other parts of the Celtic world, too, representations and tales of bizarre females abound. On the Irish Beara Penninsula, for instance, there are tales of An Chailleach Beara

(the Old Woman of Beara); in the far away North of England, legends of a fearful female figure simply known as Black Annis prevail. These were hideous crones, part witch, part savage, who dwelt in caves and ruins and whose skin and face varied in color—sometimes black, sometimes blue, sometimes green. In many instances these creatures are credited with stealing away and devouring small children. This may have represented some near-forgotten memory of ancient, evil women who, far in the past, terrorized certain communities and perhaps even carried away their young.

The Hag

The motif of the hag permeated down across the years, taking on new shapes and new identities. One of the most common forms of the crone must be an aspect of the Irish *banshee* or *bean-sidhe* (woman of the fairy). This supernatural creature often appears in three guises: a beautiful maiden, a stately matron, and an ancient hag. It is this latter incarnation that is most feared because it invariably represents age and death, and signifies the death of either the watcher or a member of his or her family. At one time, the bean-sidhe (usually in the shape of an aged crone) followed many of the great Gaelic families of Ireland, warning of approaching death and destruction. In Scotland, too, the hag motif continues with the notion of the Washer at the Ford, a particularly feared prognostication of doom. Like the sila-na-gig, this figure—that of an old woman washing blood-stained clothing by a riverbank—may well be the representation of an ancient Celtic goddess known as Clotha, who has given her name to the River Clyde. Although nothing much is known of this goddess, she is thought to have been one of the ancient embodiments of battle, who spun the cloth of life with regard to each soldier. She followed roughly the same three incarnations as the bean-sidhe and, in her last, that of the hag, washed the finished, blood-soaked material in a river, thus signifying the death of the individual concerned.

The motif translated into Irish mythology as well:

On his way to a battle, the great Ulster hero Cu-Cuchulain and three of his companions encountered an old woman, squatting by a riverside, washing the corselets of some warriors. As they approached, she kept her head turned away from them so that they could not see her face. Curious and perhaps a little terrified, the great hero asked her who she was and to give an account of herself, whereupon she turned slightly and he saw that, under her head covering, there was no face at all. And as he looked, the waters of the river where she had been washing ran red with blood. Holding up her skinny arms, the hag displayed the corselets that she'd been washing. They were those of Cuchulain's companions, although the hero's was not among them. In anger at such impertinence, he struck out at the ancient creature with his sword, but she was gone, and the blade met only empty air. Nevertheless, all his companions met their deaths in battle later that day although Cuchulain himself survived. From then on, the hero was exceptionally wary of old women, particularly of those washing clothes. However, the motif persisted, particularly in the Highlands and Islands of Scotland. It is said that the great warlord, Lachlan Mor McLean of Duart in Mull, on his way to a great feast, passed such a crone to whom he spoke sharply for some reason, although she did not respond to his anger and that within the day he was dead. His death was so unexpected that no headstone had actually been carved for him and this suddenness was attributed to the appearance of the ancient woman, believed to be a malevolent prognostication of doom.

The notion of the woman washing clothes as a symbol of death also seems to have transferred itself into the Breton motif of the Midnight Washerwomen, who were eternally condemned to wash the clothes of the unbaptized until they could find someone to take their place. Crowding around the crossroads in

Brittany, they awaited passers-by with malicious intent, ready to kill them. These washerwomen were often depicted as old and grotesque creatures, thin and emaciated to the point of being skeletal. In this form, they were to be most feared.

The figure of the crone was therefore much feared throughout the Celtic world. Indeed, there is an old Celtic saying, which ran thus: "Always avoid old women, for they have great power about them."

Like many other demonic agencies, the supernatural, nightmare crone grew out of a fusing of several myths. It was not long before the cannibalistic hag who stole away children and babies became entangled with the figure of the Washer at the Ford, with its intimations of death and destruction. These often coalesced into the terrible Welsh entity known as Gwrach y Rhibyn, roughly translated as the "Hag of the Dribble."

This dreadful creature combined many of the darker aspects of Celtic lore, including, sometimes, the drinking of blood. Descriptions of the hag varied from place to place in rural Wales. Usually, she appeared as a hunched old being, crouching down in some lonely place such as a hollow, or forest glade, her head shrouded by some sort of green covering. Beneath this was either an empty darkness (as in the Irish tale of Cuchlain) or else a countenance so hideous that it would drive a man insane just by looking at it. The "dribbles" to which the name refers may have meant saliva, which trickled from the corners of the mouth, or (as some sources said) it could mean innocent blood, which the being drank. Other accounts portray her as having only one nostril set in a hooked nose; long tusk-like teeth (some stories recount her as having a single "gobber" tooth); webbed feet and hands (in certain accounts, her hands are bird-like, resembling claws or talons); enormously long breasts; and a long and barbed tongue. In some cases, the skin was described as having a greenish tinge or being blue-grey in hue. Some of these descriptions come from Brittany, where she was known as the *Cunnere Noe*. Her hair (or what of it could be seen, peeping out from under her headcovering) was invariably long and stringy, and was usually grey in color. She was, in all respects, a ghastly-looking creature.

The Gwrach y Rhibyn

In Welsh folklore, the Gwrach y Rhibyn was somewhere between a fairy, a warning, and a vampire. She was sometimes seen at crossroads, weaving and bobbing on her ragged shawl as if waiting to attack those who passed by. At other times, she was glimpsed beside rivers or by secluded forest pools, engaged in some unseen act. At other times, she appears as a ball of light, like the flame of a candle, drifting between houses late in the evening. This is to merge the idea of the vampire/ banshee with the other Welsh notion—the *Canwyll Corph*, or *corpse candle*. This eerie phenomenon resembled either a globe of bluish-white light or else a flickering "flame" and was usually seen around graveyards and places where people had died perhaps in tragic circumstances. Corpse candles are regarded as harbingers of inevitable doom, but they are also associated with darkness and evil, so it is not inconceivable for the hag to be connected with them.

Besides warning of impending death (sometimes by wailing or keening in the old Celtic manner, although usually her very appearance was enough), the Gwrach y Rhibyn was also sometimes believed to attack individuals as they slept. She was particularly fond of small children, whose blood she drank—usually in small measure, leaving them pale, irritable, and sick. If a baby failed to thrive, in some areas it was believed that it was due to the attentions of the Hag of the Dribble. In some representations of the evil crone, her mouth is portrayed as being caked with dried blood—the blood of innocents. It is unclear as to how she drank the blood. Some legends say that it was through hollow teeth (or a hollow, gobber tooth); others say that it was with a long, barbed, dark tongue, but

none are sure. It is thought that, when it did drink blood, the creature only did so in very small quantities, returning several times to do so and allowing the victim to deteriorate slowly as if from a wasting disease—the classic vampire motif.

Besides small children, the Gwrach y Rhibyn attacked the old, who were usually unable to defend themselves against her advances. Bedridden people were especially at risk. And the most favored time for the Crone to attack was late at night and on the night of a full moon. Like certain ancient goddesses, the hag was connected to the moon and was said to draw supernatural strength from it. Thus most of the appearances occurred when the moon was high in the sky and weird shadows fell across the land. It was then that travellers on lonely roads might see an old woman crouching down near the roadside, or a flickering ball of light dogging their steps.

There are a number of tales, scattered throughout rural Wales of travellers being attacked by the hag and having to fight her off (the only means of dispelling her seems to have been by physical force) in some isolated spot. For example, from the hamlet of Llyn-y-Guelan-Goch, near Llanfor, comes a tale of a certain Reverend Pugh, a minister of religion, who managed to drive away the crone with a special stick.

There was, in times past, an ancient burial ground near the village that had a particularly sinister reputation. Strange and eerie lights were seen flickering about its fallen walls and weird sounds issued from its depths. Local people feared the place and tried to stay away from it—which was difficult, for a road ran past it, not far from the outer crumbling wall.

There was a retired minister living in the area, the Reverend Elias Pugh (though he may not have been the minister to the congregation at Llanfor and may not even have been a local man) who was regarded as very saintly and holy in his ways. It was also said that he knew a great deal about witchcraft and how to fight it. It was even said that he'd exorcised ghosts at a time. One evening, an old woman called Ann Hughes was passing by the graveyard when, looking into its depths, she thought she glimpsed what appeared to be a stooped figure moving amongst the moss-covered headstones. Like herself, the figure appeared to be that of an elderly female but it moved too quickly for her to see it clearly. In an instant it was gone, and there were only shadows moving in the cemetery under a full moon. She passed on down the road and the burial ground fell behind her.

After a while, she became aware that something seemed to be following her, and, though she was walking slowly (she was crippled with pains), it never seemed to overtake her. She attempted to quicken her step, which wasn't easy for her, but she didn't look around because she was afraid of what she might see. As she reached a crossroads, she sensed a quickening in the pace of the thing behind her and, half-turning, she saw what appeared to be a man-sized blue-white flame darting toward her. As it leapt toward her, it seemed to change into the shape of an elderly woman. (It was widely believed that in order to feed, the creature had to revert from its flame shape into a more human one). The thing looked like a Hag in an old green cloak down the front of which were dribbles of red— perhaps of blood! Ann Hughes put up a feeble resistance, but the creature was too strong for her and the victim passed into unconsciousness and fell to the road. When she recovered there was a smear of blood and a prick on her wrist, probably where the creature had drunk. (Sceptics might argue that it was a graze where she had fallen.) Gathering herself together, she hurried home and shut and bolted the door behind her. For a long time afterward, she thought that she heard the Gwrach y Rhibyn (for such she supposed it to be) moving and scraping about outside her house, trying to get in.

Over the next couple of months, many people in the community began to sicken and die, and the Gwrach y Rhibyn was seen several times in the ancient churchyard of Llyn-y-Guelan-Goch. Eventually, a deputation of locals (including Ann Hughes

herself) went to see the Godly Elias Pugh and asked him if he could do something about it. The saintly man listened to their concerns very seriously. He knew that the cemetery held some people of somewhat dubious repute and imagined that this might have attracted the creature to it. Once established within a community, the Hag of the Dribbles would be hard to remove. The only way in which he could do this, he said, was by the use of physical force: the thing would have to be driven out. Arming himself with a stout stick, the clergyman set out for the cemetery. The moon was full, and as he reached the ruined wall that surrounded the place, he thought that he glimpsed a light, weaving and moving in the gloom beyond it. As he drew nearer, he thought that, on the other side, he saw a crouching figure in a green gown from which a pale light— the glow of putrescence—flickered. He gripped the stick that he carried very tightly and walked on. He reached the wall and suddenly the moving figure in the graveyard appeared to turn to a ball of light, growing bigger and bigger, and sprang towards him. As it reached him, it seemed to turn back into a more solid shape, carrying him in front of it to the ground. He struck out with the stick, feeling it strike something solid. There was a hollow sound as if he had struck an empty drum, and the thing fell away. But suddenly it was on him again. Looking up, he saw a greasy green head-covering and, below it, almost solid darkness. The thing had no face! And yet, on the green garment that was wrapped around its thin body, there were steaks of what appeared to be dried blood. In an instant he realized that this was indeed the Gwarch y Rhibyn.

"In the Name of God, leave me be!" the holy man shouted. At the mere mention of the Holy Name, the weight of the foul thing was gone, and the Reverend Pugh was alone on the ground. He hurried home and straightway began to make preparations for his next encounter with the creature. Cutting himself another stick, he carved a small cross on the head of it and then, on the following night, he set out for the churchyard again. (It is interesting to note that, in Ireland, a staff with a similar carving was sometimes used in order to beat local witches. The same may have been true in Scotland and a number of stories from Rathlin Island—midway between the northern Irish coast and the west of Scotland mention this fact.) The light was still there, ducking and weaving amongst the grave markers and, as he approached the low wall, it moved toward him. Gradually, it coalesced into the shape of the Crone, who shot out a long black tongue in his direction. Lifting his stick, the Reverend Pugh struck it hard and the tongue was swiftly withdrawn. All the same, the Gwarch y Rhibyn continued to come at him and he lifted his cudgel and struck at it. It fell back, but then came at him again, rearing up and towering over him, its mouth opening impossibly wide. Undeterred the minister struck out again with the stick. The blow sent the creature reeling and as the clergyman advanced on it, it turned into a ball of light, almost as big as a man, and shot off across the nightbound country. It wasn't seen in that area again. This story was often told as an example of the triumph of the Church over the forces of ancient paganism.

In later times, the vampiric element of the Gwrach y Rhibyn was dropped and she simply became attached to certain old families in Wales—her appearance warning members of impending death—becoming almost like a Welsh banshee. She was now credited with wailing and keening in the traditional Irish manner, foretelling a demise or misfortune. And yet, her name—the Hag of the Dribble—hinted at her origins, the fusion of the cannibalistic crone and the harbinger of death. Maybe, even today, something evil and hungry still watches along lonely Welsh roads, waiting patiently and thirstily under a full moon.

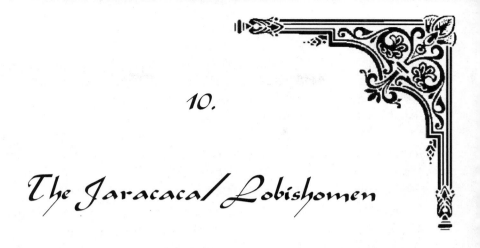

10.

The Jaracaca/Lobishomen

BRAZIL

From somewhere deep in the leafy canopy of the Brazilian jungle comes a thin, high-pitched, coughing roar that is said to be the cry of a *Jaracaca*. The eerie cry often sends a shiver through those who hear it and know what it means, for the Jaracaca is greatly feared everywhere in Brazil.

It is difficult to understand how Jaracacas come into existence. Are they the souls of the departed in some other form, or are they, in fact, demons that dwell in the jungles? The answer isn't clear. Some legends say that they are little more than a coalescence of the darkness deep in the forest, which has taken on a life of its own and is hostile to mankind. For others, they

are the remnants of old, blood-drinking gods who were worshipped in South America hundreds of years ago. And yet others still hold that they are the spirits of evil people, somehow denied entry into both heaven and hell, and forced to lived in the deepest jungle, taking what sustenance they can.

The Jaracaca is a curious form of vampire. It certainly drinks some blood—although the amount of blood it takes is not great, leading to a continual weakness rather than death for its victim. It also drinks milk, particularly human milk from nursing mothers. In order to do this, the Jaracaca adopts the form of a great snake that slides through the jungle unobserved, approaching mothers who are breastfeeding their babies. Unbeknownst to the mother, the snake inserts itself between the baby and the breast-nipple, and continues to drink the milk. In order to silence the baby, it shoves its tail into the infant's mouth. If it enjoys the taste of the milk, it will return again and again, thus depriving the child of nourishment and leaving it thin and hungry.

When confronted, it is believed in some parts of Brazil, that the Jaracaca (still in its snake-like guise) can spit peculiar and terrible venom, which can produce an almost instant insanity from which there is no recovery. Occasionally, the Jaracaca will drink blood from the upper arms of sleeping men, but it will only do this when human milk is not available. To do this, it will slide into a hut, in the guise of a snake, and encircle the upper arm of the sleeper before feeding. As it feeds, its secretions also produce insanity in its victim, so that he wakes in the morning as a raving madman. For this reason, the attentions of the creature are greatly feared, and prayers and incantations are offered up before going to sleep.

Protection From the Jaracaca

There is no known way in which to destroy a Jaracaca, so your best bet is avoidance or some form of protection. Amongst certain Brazilians, ancient spells and talismans are probably the best form of defense, although prayers to Catholic saints are also considered effective. The blessing of a Catholic priest is considered to be a defense against such vampires, though whether this is as good as the spell of the jungle shaman is a matter that is open to question. A blessing or an incantation should be delivered before a child is breastfed to ensure that the infant actually gets its mother's milk.

The Lobishomen

Throughout Brazil, vampires come in many forms, of which the Jaracaca is only one. All of them appear in differing shapes, reflecting the cultural influences that have formed the country itself. For example, another vampiric entity is the *lobishomen*, which bears little resemblance to the Jaracaca and which, although it also attacks mainly women, seems to have different imperatives. Indeed, the lobishomen actually *looks* different. Humanoid in form, the vampire is little over 2 inches high and resembles a furry, bald-headed monkey with a wizened, evil face. The feet of the lobishomen are large and full, almost like plush slippers, which adds to its silence and stealth as it moves about. Its name is slightly confusing because another lobishomen appears in Portuguese folklore—this time, to denote a full-grown werewolf-type creature.

The Brazilian name probably reflects Portuguese influence in the country, especially when one remembers that, in Brazil, anyone who has formerly been a werewolf in life is certain to become a lobishomen after death. This vampire entity, however, does not kill its victims—all of whom are women—but, like the Jaracaca, takes only a small amount of

blood for its sustenance. Again, like the Jaracaca, there is a substance in its saliva that has an effect upon the women it attacks, turning them into nymphomaniacs. And the lobishomen attacks only at night and when its victims are asleep or dozing so that they are roused as sexual predators. In fact, no amount of sex can gratify them and, for long periods, they will have relations with any man who comes near to them. In many communities, this makes the lobishomen a very popular type of vampire amongst the male inhabitants, and so little effort is made to destroy it. Indeed, the creature is actually *encouraged* to visit villages through magical incantations designed to lure it there. All males are, of course, safe in the knowledge that the vampire will not attack them; however, all women, no matter what age they are, fear the being.

The Pishtaco

Few descriptions exist of a much more widely feared vampire creature known as the *pishtaco*. Like most other Brazilian vampires, it operates under the cover of night and when its victims are asleep. Although not strictly a Brazilian vampire (the pishtaco is native to Peru), elements of such a being are to be found in some remote areas of the country. Again, this is a curious vampire, as it does not initially drink blood. In Peru and in certain regions of Brazil, the creature first nourishes itself on the fat and semen of the sleeper. Only when it has gorged itself on these (or when it is exhausted) will it commence to drink blood. And then it may drink the vital fluid in copious amounts.

In Peru, there is no real description of the pishtaco but, in its Brazilian form (where it occurs), it may sometimes take the guise of a bat. (It is interesting to note that in many of the Hollywood films, Dracula—an East European nobleman— can take the guise of a vampire bat. Such creatures do not exist in Eastern Europe, the vampire bat being native to South America, and it is this form that the pishtaco sometimes takes in order to enter houses and attack sleepers.) In this guise, it attacks the soles of the feet, drawing off quantities of fat and blood and leaving the sleeper weak and debilitated. Unlike either the Jaracaca or the lobishomen it will attack either men or women, and, as this vampire drinks semen, men are particularly at risk.

The Asema and Witchcraft

As in many other parts of the world, vampirism in both Central and South America often has strong connections with witchcraft. In fact, throughout Brazil, witches are largely considered to be blood-drinking entities in their own right, travelling about after dark to attack their enemies and those who are considered to be "good people" (Catholic churchgoers and clerics are considered to be especially at risk from these creatures). In order to do so, they assume the form of balls of light, which can travel at fantastic speeds. Such balls are usually seen during the hours of darkness when most people are asleep and the powers of the witches are at their height.

Throughout much of Brazil, witches and vampires are often confused with each other, and one of the main types of vampire is the *asema*, a kind of "living vampire" that usually takes the form of an old man or an old woman during daylight hours. As soon as darkness falls, however, it assumes the form of a blinding ball of light, which travels over the countryside in search of victims. Once it has found one, the asema immediately reverts to solid form once more in order to feed. Once sated, it assumes the guise of a light-ball again to return to its home, where it resumes a seemingly human life. In some instances, the asema can actually remove its skin, like a coat, to become the light-ball, which can then

move at a fantastic speed. In order to feed, the being can take its human form or it can remain as a light-ball, although in this latter form it does not drink blood as such but rather draws off the energy and vitality from those sleepers whom it encounters.

Just to confuse matters even further, the light of which these flying balls were composed often varied in color, depending upon how dangerous the entity was. Some accounts describe the asema as a ball of pale, shimmering light of indeterminate color. These beings were not the most dangerous but, if they attended a sleeper over a prolonged period of time, the results could be serious, even fatal. Other descriptions recount the color as deep red, and these are even more dangerous. But more deadly still are balls of deep blue or aquamarine light. Such entities cannot be sated and will leave their victims ill and debilitated. Many of these can take on a physical, human form—though not necessarily their own—and will appear briefly as beautiful maidens or handsome men. However, the vampire cannot maintain such a guise for very long and will usually revert either to its older form or to a ball of light, which will then shoot off at great speed.

Old men or old women living alone, either at a village edge or deep in the jungle, are always suspected of being asema, particularly if they are somewhat reclusive and strange in their ways. Locals, especially children who are most at risk from the attentions of the vampire, are taught to make certain secret and furtive signs when meeting them on a road or a path in order to ward away the evil that resides in them and to divert attention. However, if such an old person shows an undue interest in an individual, it is a sign that he or she has been "picked out" by the asema (the living vampire) and that he or she will have a visit from one before many nights are past.

Remedies and Precautions

If a person is suspected of being attacked by an asema, there are certain remedies and precautions that he or she can use. For example, a potential victim can eat certain combinations of herbs—which, interestingly enough, include garlic—that will "taint the blood" and render it foul to the vampire. Another defense mechanism is to lay a good number of small white stones or seeds from various plants outside one's door. As with the Eastern European vampire, the asema are considered to be obsessive creatures and will not enter a house until all the stones and sees have been arranged, neatly and tidily, into piles. This will take the most of the night and, at sunrise, the asema must return to its home to rest; consequently, its prospective victim is spared.

Another way to destroy or inhibit the asema as it travels through the countryside as a ball of light is to find the skin that it has discarded. This is usually somewhere in the house that it has inhabited in its human form, and whoever finds it has the vampire in his or her power. Should the skin-cloak be destroyed, the creature itself ceases to exist. The ball of light, which is the essence of the being, will simply fizzle out and disappear. The best way to destroy the skin, it is said, is to burn it and to scatter the ashes through the forest so that it cannot be reassembled again by magic. However, some magicians keep the skin themselves so that the vampire is their slave and can be used against their enemies. As long as the magician holds the skin, the vampire is in his or her power, but the creature (who is also a magician) is tricky and might devise ways of getting its "cloak" back, to the detriment of its captor.

The Iara

Closely related to the asema are the *Iara*, or *mboiacu*, which dwell deep in the Brazilian jungles. Folklorists have

sometimes argued that these creatures are really the same and that both names refer to a type of shape-changing witch. Some Brazilians have suggested that the name mboiacu is simply an ancient Tupi word meaning "a sorcerer who can take the form of a snake." The vampire glides through the jungle in its serpent form, attacking anyone it encounters or crosses its path. Its eyes are said to be extremely red and almost hypnotic; its stare is capable of freezing its victims to the spot.

At other times it can take the form of a beautiful young woman with a sweet singing voice who can lure male travellers deeper into the jungle, like the *lorelli* of ancient mythology. Once she has lured her victims to her, she will revert to her serpent form in order to feed, wrapping herself round her victims and drawing blood and semen from them with her fangs. Her song is very lovely and, like the cry of the Jaracaca, it can be heard all through the jungle, often drawing men away from their work or from other duties. They are powerless to resist and may follow the siren song into the deep jungle where the Iara is waiting for them. There are, however, a number of protective chants that can be uttered as soon as a potential victim hears the song that will nullify its powers. But these must be said extremely quickly by the person involved, before the hypnotic spell takes hold.

There is much debate as to whether the Iara is actually one of the Undead or a living person. Some authorities assert that it is the spirit of someone who has died violently or before their time, or, as Christianity spread across Brazil, who has died outside the Church and whose body has been buried in the jungle. Others state that it is a living magician, male or female, who has sold his or her soul to the Devil (a later

Christian concept) and who lives apart from the rest of the community. Whatever the nature of the creature, it is greatly feared, especially among those with Tupi blood in their veins.

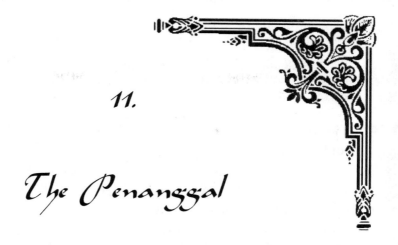

11.

The Penanggal

MALAYSIA

ere in the West, we are well used to the traditional image of the vampire—that of a tall, saturnine man in a cape, or a beautiful woman in a flimsy, flowing gown. At least that is the creature that the Hollywood film sets have created. Even in folklore, the traditional vampiric form is that of a walking corpse—an entire body risen out of the grave. In some regions of the East, however, the perception of the vampire may be a little different and not so clear-cut.

It is believed, for instance, that some Eastern vampires can detach certain body parts, which they can send out to carry out their blood-drinking activities. In some parts of China, for example, it was once believed that the hands of corpses (particularly the right hand) could wander about at night, attacking sleepers and drinking both blood and semen through the fingernails. In Vietnam and parts of Cambodia,

too, the detached head of a cadaver floated through the air, with antennae extending from its nose, drinking the blood of the unwary. Parts of the body, it seems, can be almost as virulent as the entire body itself.

Confusion is also created by the belief that not all vampires may be dead. As in some parts of Africa, Asia, and Eastern Europe, the idea of a "living vampire" prevails. Vampirism and the drinking of blood is strongly associated with witchcraft, and it is thought that some magicians either travel is the guise of animals or else send parts of their body in order to fulfil their evil designs. And, just to confuse matters, it is also believed that sorcerers can often raise bodies from the dead and command them to do their bidding. Whether they used the entire body or a part of the body was up to the sorcerer, but such beings could drink blood or spread disease. Malaysia was a case in point for many of these vampires.

Traits of the Penanggal

One of the most common forms of the Undead there was the *penanggal*, or *penanggalan*. This was a ghastly being—little more than a floating head, which trailed entrails and a still-beating heart behind it as it flew through the air in search of victims. It was usually the head of a woman who had died in childbirth, a time when it was believed that many women were susceptible to sorcery. Sometimes, the head was controlled simply by a hostile spirit and, in other instances, by a malignant sorcerer. This creature travelled at night, and its victims consisted of small children or pregnant women. It was said that the penanggal operated out of spite and jealousy, but that it might also attack on the instructions of an evil magician. The penanggal might attack children when they were still in the womb or just after they had been born, drawing their blood and reducing them to little more than a husk. It flew with a loud screaming noise to announce its presence, its mouth caked with dried blood and its ghastly entrails floating after it through the air. When it had fed, it was assumed, the being would return and rejoin the rest of its body to rest until its next foray.

Destroying the Penanggal

The best way to destroy a penanggal was to catch it by the floating entrails and seize the heart. Alternatively, it could be lured onto a bush, where the entrails would be caught. The trick was to prevent the head from reconnecting with the body. Because the penanggal was a creature of the night and only travelled during the hours of darkness, it could not exist for long in the sunlight but would shrivel away and die. If the still-beating heart could be stopped, the vampire's life would certainly come to an end.

This remedy was, of course, highly dangerous because the penanggal was extremely vicious and would attack anyone who tried to hinder it. Its teeth were incredibly strong and its eyes could shoot hellish fire at its assailant if necessary. In some areas of Malaya, it was believed that the creature could spit deadly venom that could paralyze anyone who sought to capture it, rendering them immobile. Moreover, it could emit a piercing scream, which could stun anyone close to it. Having stunned its victim with the sound of its cry, the head would then feed on the blood before flying back to rejoin its body.

A less dangerous but less satisfactory way of destroying the vampire was to try to find the lower half of its body and stop the flying head from returning to it. This might involve entombing the headless corpse in some form of container or box. However, if the head was under the command of some evil magician, sorcery might be used to open the container, and the two parts of the body would be reunited. Or, it was even believed, the penanggal might be able to turn itself into smoke and enter the container or chest of its own volition. Although

this was considered the safest way to trap and destroy a penanggal, it was therefore considered rather unsatisfactory.

The Pontipinnak

The scream of the penanggal allied it to another type of vampire known throughout Malaysia called the *pontipinnak*. Descriptions of this type of vampire vary—some describe it as a corpse, some as a floating head similar to the penanggal, others as a living being—but on one thing they all agree, this creature could transform itself into a screech owl and in this form might emit a cry that could either stun or paralyze. Like the penanggal, the pontipinnak is a creature of the night and can only be encountered during hours of darkness. Strong sunlight could immobilize this vampire, and long exposure to the sun's rays would ultimately destroy it. And again, like the penanggal, the pontipinnak's victims were babies, small children, and old people, as well as pregnant women.

The Langsuir

To confuse matters further, in some regions of Malaysia, the pontipinnak is considered to be a variation of *langsuir*, another form of vampiric creature that thrived on the blood of newborn babies. This creature is often described as a tall, graceful, and beautiful woman, always dressed in green and with jet-black hair, exceptionally long fingernails, and slitted cat-like eyes. She did not walk but simply glided to her victims as though floating above the ground. This is not a flying head, but a complete woman, although in certain villages it is thought that she can detach parts of her body—especially her hands with their long nails, which could injure a victim and draw blood—and use them independently of the main body. It was also believed that this vampire could take the form of a small insect, cricket, or buzzing fly.

Both the pontipinnak and the langsuir are believed to be the spirits of women who have died in childbirth and who operate out of a sense of bitterness and jealousy against the living, or else under the direct and malefic influence of a sorcerer. They can be driven away by specific incantations, but these can only be carried out by a particularly powerful magician. An alternative method of disposal is to find the sorcerer who is controlling the vampire and to force him or her to remove the spell.

The Bajang

A Malaysian vampire that was just as dangerous as the penanggal and was strongly associated with malefic sorcery was the *bajang*. This was not a vampire that had formerly been a living person but was a creature specifically *created* by magic in order to do harm. This creature, it is believed, was created

by sorcery from the remnants of a stillborn baby and was motivated by the whim and desire of the controlling magician. Like the langsuir or pontipinnak, this vampire could take a number of animal forms, most commonly that of a cat. However, unlike these two creatures, the bajang was usually of a male gender and its victims were usually women, sometimes pregnant (in which case it magically attacked the child in the womb), but not always. It was particularly rapacious and hungry after nightfall and could be sent out on missions of destruction as soon as the moon was up. Once it had attacked its victim and had drawn off some of its blood, it would return to its master to rest in a box or chest that the sorcerer had hidden away. In this animal guise, the bajang could also spread sickness and disease throughout a community. It might also bring great personal misfortune to individuals whom the sorcerer wished to injure. The only way to destroy such a creature was to hunt down the sorcerer concerned and force him or her to "unmake" it through magic and incantations. As a precaution, stillborn fetuses were burned to prevent their falling into the hands of such magicians.

The Polong

A similar type of Malaysian vampire is the *polong*. This is also a *created* vampire, manufactured by evil magicians. It is made by capturing blood in a bottle with a long, thin neck, over which spells and incantations are then uttered. The bottle is then stored away to incubate and, after about six or seven days, the polong emerged. As with many other Malaysian vampires, descriptions of it usually vary. In some instances it was described simply as a red-skinned floating head (a little like the penanggal); neither male nor female; and with a long, sharp, hollow tongue, through which it drank the blood and semen of its victims. However, the most common description was that of a small female figure, no more than an inch tall, which could enter a house through the smallest of chinks and attack those within it. When it had feasted, the polong invariably returned to its bottle, in which it rested and which had to be kept away from strong sunlight in a secret place. Whilst it was being "birthed," the polong had to be fed with blood—this was carried out in a rather gruesome manner. The magician had to cut off a finger from either his or her own hand or from the hand of a victim and place it in the neck of the bottle for the growing polong to suck. From time to time, if it had not ventured forth (and only the magician could release it from its bottle), the polong had to be nourished with fresh human blood. This could be from a cut in the magician's own body or from warm blood that he or she had procured for the purpose.

The Pelesit

In some cases, the polong was accompanied by another sort of vampire, the *pelesit*. This was also a "created" creature, made by magic from the tongue of a stillborn baby. In a sense, it was a "forerunner," or herald, of the polong, usually entering a house first to prepare the way by spreading disease and sickness, and sometimes insanity as well. In most cases, the pelesit takes the form of a house cricket or fly and is regarded somewhere as a cross between a demon and a vampiric entity. It drank blood, particularly from open cuts or wounds, but this was not its primary purpose—that was to spread misery and unhappiness, and to debilitate individuals in advance of the polong's attentions. As did the polong, it had to be sustained with procured blood (or sometimes it could also be sustained by feeding on small amounts of saffron rice) and could be entrapped by charms and spells. Under direct magical questioning, both the polong and pelesit might be forced to reveal the names of the sorcerers who had created them, although, in this instance, one had to be careful because if the magic used was not strong enough, the vampire might remain silent or

even lie. There was no real formal way of destroying either entity without the help of the magician who had created them.

The Line Between Vampire and Demon

In many parts of Malaysia and in Burma, the distinction between vampire and demon was extremely blurred. For example, it was sometimes believed that the pelesit could actually *possess* people at the behest of the controlling sorcerer, making them do things which they would not ordinarily do. They might, for example, vomit green bile or sing bawdy songs or even, on occasion, drink blood themselves. This was a sure sign that they were possessed by an evil spirit. Nor was there any way of driving the evil from them—a number of incantations and spells might be tried but, generally speaking, the polong and pelesit spirits were far too strong. Once again, the only person who could "unmake" them was the magician who had created them. Only in this way could their evil be lifted.

Throughout Malaysia, it is said, spirits and demons lurk everywhere, sometimes invisibly, waiting to fall on unsuspecting victims and turning them into demonic or vampiric creatures. The diversity of such creatures reflected the difference in the peoples and beliefs that comprise Malaysia. Amongst the Chewong, however, there remains, even today, an extremely strong belief in a lurking vampire known as the *maneden*. This vampire lurks amongst the leaves of the wild pandanus plant and attacks only humans who cut or harm this plant in some way. Very small, to the point of invisibility, it attaches itself either to the elbow of a man or to the nipple of a woman, where it draws blood, leaving its victim weak and listless. The only way to stop or divert its attentions is to give it a substitute, usually an oily nut from the hodj nut tree. For this reason, certain Chewong members carry nuts or sweets with them when they go on a journey, lest they inadvertently damage a pandanus plant.

Of course, the maneden was not the only demonic vampire that lurked in the Malaysian forests and jungles. The *eng banka*, for instance, is the ghost of a dog that had died or had been accidentally killed somewhere away from human habitation. Its spirit inhabited certain trees and could be used by magicians to work evil against their enemies. The being (which is never fully described or which had numerous descriptions) dwells mainly in swampy areas and was considered to be very dangerous. Like the pelesit, it could spread illness and insanity. There is no known cure for its attentions, although certain charms and spells could lessen its effects.

Even though Malaysian vampires were rather numerous and often took fantastic and grotesque shapes, the world of the Eastern vampire still remains shrouded in mystery as far as the West is concerned. Films depicting vampires are usually centred around the comfortable stereotypical Western imagery. There have, however, been attempts to introduce such creatures as the penanggal into Western vampire lore, usually without much success. For example, in 1956 the Malaysian Cathay-Keris Productions released the film *Pontiannak*. In this, a woman who sucked the blood of her husband who had been bitten by a snake was turned into the vampiric entity of the title. The film was not a great success, but during the late 1950s and early 1960s, Cathay-Keris released a number of films featuring the pontiannak, and hinting at Malaysian vampire lore to the American market. Most enjoyed moderate success but were promptly forgotten; the others were box-office flops. It seems that we are more comfortable with the man in the dark cloak than the flying ghoulish head. And yet, deep in the Malaysian forests, who knows what ancient evil might still be lurking?

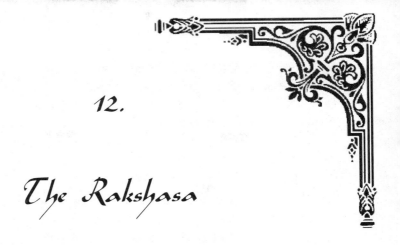

12.

The Rakshasa

INDIA

In many instances, the concept of vengeance is strong in vampire lore. In many cultures, the dead simply returned either to right some wrong that had been done against them in life, or else to take their revenge upon the perpetrator of that wrong. Such a wrong might be actual or imagined, for the dead often behaved like the living and sometimes acted just as irrationally. The dead were to be respected and feared.

In certain countries, the the idea malicious dead was sometimes tied up with religion. For example, a child who had the impertinence (or misfortune) to be born during a religious festival might come back as a hostile revenant after death. In some cases, the blame for giving birth to a child during a holy time fell upon the infant's mother, and so the curse of returning as a vengeful corpse often fell upon her. This was particularly

true in the East where, in some male-dominated societies, women sometimes held a slightly different (sometimes more lowly) status than they did in the West. Many of the Eastern demons were, therefore, female and many of them were incredibly hostile toward males.

The concept of vengeance from beyond the grave and the notion of a dark female spirit came together in Indian myth. Here, the unquiet dead, usually female (though not always), wandered through the cemeteries, seeking to do harm to any who crossed their paths. These were known as *rakshasa* (the word means "injurer"), who sought to waylay travellers and harm them. The term is, however, a confusing one because, although it can refer to a vampire, it can also refer to a wider class of malignant Hindu demons, which display both male and female characteristics. And just to add a further confusion, the vampiric rakasha are divided into a number of subgroups, with the term simply being a general category.

The Churels

There were, for example, the *churels*. These were the spirits of women who had died whilst giving birth during the Devali Festival, one of the most important celebrations in the Hindu calendar. Descriptions of these creatures vary according to the region of India where they are found. In some areas, they are portrayed as beautiful women, their heads covered, carrying a lantern. They prowl graveyards, attempting to lure in passers-by. Localized folklore states that are very beautiful and they are temptresses, which few men can resist. The sight of eerie lights moving through a cemetery is probably enough to make travellers give such places a wide berth, however. In other areas, the churels wait by the roadside, still in the guise of beautiful maidens, calling to wayfarers in an attempt to seduce them. Once they had the travellers in their clutches, they drew off their blood and semen, and discarded them as though they were withered husks. In other folktales, the churel was a hideous creature totally naked, though still completely female. They were described as having pig's faces with huge fangs, terrible rending claw-like hands, sagging breasts, a pot-belly, and long and untidy pubic hair. Hardly the beautiful damsel with her lantern! They were said to dwell within the tombs of the cemeteries, coming out after dark to attack people living close by. In yet other accounts the being had a vaguely human face but with great lips and razor-sharp teeth, which it used to consume the flesh of its victims as well as drink their blood. The variance in descriptions probably arises out of the confusion between the walking dead—those who had once been alive and human—and wholly demonic entities.

The Pisacas

Another type of rakshasa was known as the *pisacas*. This form of malignant entity often maintained a state of invisibility, but the effects of its attentions were all too apparent. These beings usually lingered around places where prayer or religious observances were carried on and did their best to disrupt them. They did so by making rude noises or by shouting. More dangerously, however, they caused a kind of lethargy to fall over the participants, leaving them weak and unfocused on their meditations. In extreme situations, those taking part in prayer might die because of the pisacas' attentions. In some folktales, the simple shouting of the word *Uncle* would drive them away; however, the origins of this belief remain unknown. Most of the pisacas are female and, in former times, their screeching often interrupted holy teachings given by holy men, to confuse and tire his listeners. In order to cause part of this disruption, however, they have to assume a visible shape and are therefore identified as pisacas. These rakshasas had a particular antipathy toward holiness and this, once again, showed their possible links to Hindu demonic forces.

Certain rakshasa were said to have adapted more subtle ways of attacking human communities. They lodged themselves in the water supply of a town or settlement and gradually made the people waste away as if by an illness (in some areas this was said to be another aspect of the pisacas). Those who died became rakshasa themselves. It was believed that this type of rakshasa had an extremely gaunt, almost skeletal appearance and that they also sometimes lurked about the entrances of graveyards and cemeteries, ready to attack those who came and went from such places. It was also thought that this form of rakshasa could possess a mourner (usually the last one to leave a graveyard after an interment) or that they were powerful magicians and could make mourners commit crimes against their will. In some districts, they were believed to be corpse eaters and had long black teeth with their hair standing on end, as if electrified.

The Geyal

The most dangerous of all the rakshasas were the *geyal*, or *gayal*. These were actually vengeful spirits (usually female) who attacked the living simply for their own malicious pleasure and might well drink their blood or eat their flesh. They were somewhere between ghosts and demons, and were originally believed to be the spirits of those against whom a great wrong had been committed when they were alive, and who had now turned against all humankind. Later, it was believed that this was simply the vengeful spirit of someone who had not been buried properly (that is, not according to Hindu ritual) and was taking revenge on his or her relatives. As demons could, they could sometimes possess individuals—usually entering their bodies through the mouths whilst they were eating. They were especially attracted to pregnant women. Once in possession of a body, they could draw the good from it from within, causing the person to sicken and waste away.

Those whom they initially attacked were often related to them in some way, but gayal could also disrupt the wider community if they had a mind to. There was really no way of destroying this type of rakshasa—the best way of dealing with them was prevention and so proper funeral rites according to Hindu custom had to be strictly observed.

Minor Rakshasa

A number of other minor rakshasa also threatened mankind in various ways. Foremost amongst these were the *bhuta*, vicious, demonic entities with long, lolling, black tongues that supernaturally drew the essence from individuals through the bizarre method of eating their excrement. If attacked, such creatures would retaliate by killing their victims, slitting them open with razor-sharp talons, and devouring their intestines.

Another type of rakshasa, the *bramaparush*, also had an appetite for human intestines, wrapping them around its body and performing a ritualistic dance. Another vampiric entity, the *jigarkhwar*, found in the Sind area of India, was attracted, not by intestines, but by blood and liver, which it consumed after paralyzing its victim with a mesmeric stare that couldn't be avoided no matter how hard the prey tried to look away. There were a number of other blood-drinking, flesh-eating creatures in other parts of India, most of them reflecting the confusion that exists in the Indian mind between vampires and formal demons.

And, just to confuse matters even further, some beliefs claim that the vampires are not reanimated corpses at all but the emanations of living people—usually powerful and malignant magicians or witches. In fact, in some areas of the country the word *rakshasa* simply means "sorcerer"— many of whom were connected with animals and animal spirits, particularly owls and tigers. Such magicians could operate over long distances, easily drawing the health and vitality from their victims

even though they were nowhere near them. And, as already mentioned, some of the rakshasa travelled about invisibly and could possess people at the meal-table or when asleep. They are a kind of demon, totally opposed to everything that is human, and have never actually been alive.

Ravana

It is also believed that the rakshasa might have been a king or leader. This is Ravana, who was considered to be the arch-rakshasa and lord of the Undead. He is described as having 10 heads, 20 arms, and fiercely burning eyes. Moreover, he was an extremely skilful shapeshifter, adapting a number of guises as diverse as a rock, a corpse, a puff of smoke, or a swirl of dust. He was also considered to be practically invulnerable. It is said that he could break mountains with his bare hands, create storms at sea with a puff of his breath, and reduce a man to dust simply by drawing his soul from him. Ravana

was also considered to be the ultimate vampire, consumed by a desire for human blood.

According to Hindu legend, Ravana was born into a universe filled with terrible screaming and shrieking noises. The offspring of a voracious female demon and a Hindu holy man whom she had tempted, Ravana gained much dark power through contemplation and meditation that lasted for many thousands of years. He then approached Brahma and asked him for the gift of immortality, but the god, suspicious of Ravana's motives, refused. Ravana pressed his argument and eventually a compromise was reached: Ravana would be immune from all elements in the material world. However, he scoffed at the idea of needing protection from the puny humans who inhabited this plane of existence and vowed that he would eradicate them. He was now virtually indestructible. When one of his 10 heads was cut off, for instance, it grew back again almost immediately.

In order to fulfil his threat of human eradication, he developed an insatiable taste for human blood and sought it out at every available opportunity, killing with impunity. But although he had made Ravana almost invulnerable, Brahma had left a loophole in his supernatural armour. Although much of his body was invulnerable, his heart was not, and it was into this that the Hindu hero Rama fired an arrow to slay the monster. But, although he was slain and left to rot, Ravana was revived by human blood, supplied by various rakshasa from all across India and, because, he had been slain by a mortal, vowed revenge on all humankind.

He instructed his followers to double their efforts to slay humans and to drink their blood and devour their internal organs. He further instructed them that whenever possible they were to spread harmful and painful diseases throughout the communities so that people would die in the thousands. Such was his revenge against Rama and his kind. Once more, the idea of supernatural idea of vengeance is fulfilled.

Kali

Other legends, however, say that the rakshasa are *not* the followers of Ravana but are in fact emanations of Kali, the Hindu goddess of death. This fearsome entity is herself a manifestation of the "Dark Mother," the goddess Durga (whose name means "inaccessible"), and she was popularly worshipped throughout the sixth and seventh centuries. Kali has four arms: in one hand she carries a sword, and in another, the head of a slain demon; the other two are raised in blessing. She wears a necklace of human skulls and a girdle made out of human hands—her face and breasts are covered in blood. It seems reasonable that this fearsome and ghoulish goddess would be connected with the rakshasa who travel throughout the countryside killing people and supplying Kali with blood and dead human flesh upon which some believe she subsists.

Repelling the Rakshasa

It is not only human beings, however, that rakshasa are interested in. They will also devour horses and cattle, which are essential to community life. An attack of the rakshasa can devastate a village and destroy a community (often in a single night). And there is little that can be done to drive them away. Fire, however, is a potent deterrent. According to most holy teaching, all the Undead fear the purifying fire, and it is the only thing that will drive them away. However, applying this remedy can be difficult because many rakshasa, especially the pisacas, often go about invisibly. Prayer and meditation or saying some part of holy Scripture tends to upset them and drives them away, but they will usually return after a time. The only effective way to dispel rakshasa is through a special exorcism known only to certain holy men, which involves the burning of certain sacred herbs and chanting holy names. Even then, it is doubtful as to whether the rakshasa can be *completely* dispelled, but this should be enough to halt their activities for a long time.

When a community is suffering from rakshasa attacks, it is perhaps wise to visit the sites of recent burials. If the soil of one of the graves has been disturbed, it is usually a certain sign of rakshaka activity, and the spot should be opened. The grave is more than likely to contain a female, because it is women who are more susceptible to becoming rakshasa. The body will be more florid and "fresh-looking" than a normal corpse—a telltale sign that it is one of the Undead—although the final diagnosis can only be made by a holy man or teacher. The body must then be burned, although the spirit will still be free. Those who witness the cremation must be careful not to breathe in the smoke, for they will be possessed by the rakshasa and, in turn, become one of the Undead themselves. One should also be careful not to let embers from the fire fall near animals, because the rakshasa have a special affinity for creatures and birds (particularly cats and owls) and may enter into their bodies in order to attack humans. When the body is completely consumed by the fire, the ashes must be gathered up and buried deep in the earth while prayers are said over the resting place. The spot where these ashes are buried must be avoided forever in case the essence of the rakshasa still lingers there, ready to overcome the unwary traveller.

In India, the notions of the Undead are mixed with belief in demons and gods, and have been incorporated into legend and mythology. The picture that emerges is a confusing and complex one—filled with various vampiric forms, of possession, and with supernatural deities. Perhaps somewhere in dim and distant Indian history there may be some point of origin—some single and incredibly ancient figure that combines all these elements—but today, who can say?

13.

The Sampiro

ALBANIA

In some parts of the world, the notion of difference plays a large part in vampire belief. Those who are strange, who do not readily fit into the overall community, or who have odd ways about them must be supernatural creatures. Tied in with this is a kind of *xenophobia*—the fear and suspicion of the stranger, especially if that stranger is of a different ethnic origin.

An example of how difference plays a central role in the vampire belief of a region is found in the figure of the Albanian *sampiro* (also sometimes known in parts of Albania and Montenegro as the *liugat*). Although coming from an area of the world where there is a rich, cultural vampiric mix, the sampiro is nevertheless a fantastic and unique creature. In Albania, it is believed that anyone who is born to Turkish parentage is destined to become a vampire and that in a vampiric

state, they will take the form of sampiro. A long history of mistrust and suspicion exists between the Albanians and the Turks, dating back to the time of the Turkish Ottoman Empire, and perhaps the belief reflects this.

Traits of the Sampiro

As a vampire entity, the sampiro is a somewhat bizarre creature. Descriptions of it vary in minor details from region to region, but its basic characteristics remain constant throughout Albania. Swathed in its grave shroud or in voluminous flowing garments, which hide most of its body, the sampiro goes about after nightfall, following it victims. Two things are very noticeable: firstly, it wears incredibly high heels, which make it totter and sway as it moves; and secondly, its eyes are large and luminous and peer through the garments in which it is swathed in a most alarming manner. (Some accounts suggest that they might be as big as car headlights.) As it follows its victim, the sampiro makes kissing sounds—these are said to be the creature pursing its lips in anticipation of drinking blood. The thought of a bizarre figure, covered in material, stumbling along on high heels and "blowing kisses" may seem extremely humorous, but is greeted with some awe and terror in Albania.

In effect, the sampiro is more of a pest than a threat. The amount of blood that it takes from its victims is minimal, leaving them weak and torpid rather than dead, although, over a period of time, the attentions of the creature *can* result in fatality. However, the sight of a shroud-swathed figure with large and luminous eyes bearing down is enough to terrify even the bravest of individuals. There is an added eerie element, as the sampiro is not only abroad during the hours of darkness, but it also seems to prefer fog and is usually abroad on foggy evenings. Mist and shadow add to the feelings of mystery and terror that surround the creature. The sound of its high heels

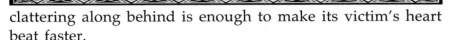

clattering along behind is enough to make its victim's heart beat faster.

It is not only Turks who become sampiro when they die, although many of the vampires were originally of that nationality. Albanians who have committed unusual or unnatural acts can also rise from their tombs as members of the Undead. People who have had sex with animals are also certain of becoming vampires, as are homosexuals and transvestites. Men who have married or had sex with Turkish women are also at risk, as are those who have frequented prostitutes, no matter what their nationality. Those who have eaten meat that has previously been handled by a Turk (sometimes by *any* foreigner) or those who have attended a Moslem service may also join the ranks of the sampiro. In certain areas, it is also believed that liars and thieves might also become vampires.

Not long after such people have been buried—usually no more than about three or four days—they rise again and go tottering about through the dark and fog. In some parts of Albania, it is thought that the sampiro may carry some of the earth from its grave in its navel, but this may be to confuse it with a creature known as an *olgolgen*, a vampire from the Czech Republic. This is a much more ferocious entity who can kill those whom it attacks unless they can grab and scatter the graveyard earth, an action that prevents the sampiro's returning to its tomb.

It is possible to argue that the idea of the sampiro might have been used to maintain the purity of the Albanian people, and also to keep a sense of morality and propriety amongst them. The idea of tramping along fog-bound roads in high heels and wrapped in a winding sheet or some other garment, driven by an insatiable lust for blood, is probably enough to keep most Albanians on a strictly moral path and to keep them from marrying or having relationships with those from outside their own ethnic group. The sampiro, then, acts as a kind of supernatural "bogeyman" to keep wayward individuals in line and to keep foreigners out.

Destroying the Sampiro

The best way to destroy a sampiro is, allegedly, by staking it. All of us are probably familiar with staking—driving a stake into the heart of a vampire—from our reading of Bram Stoker's *Dracula*. The practice, however, is not universally used as a method of vampire disposal, and it is only popular in some parts of Eastern Europe and Russia. Even here, it is considered to be rather unreliable. Firstly, the wood of which the stake is made needs to be considered. For instance, the Russian *oupir* (a particularly vicious vampiric entity) can be disposed of by staking it, but the stake has to be made of yew (as swords were in some parts of Ireland—see the legend of Abhartach, page 64), whereas in other parts of Russia, the stake must be made from oak or ash. In Hungary, the stake must be made of mountain ash or rowan. The wrong sort of wood, therefore, renders the staking ineffective. Furthermore, if the stake were to be removed from its resting place at any time, warn certain East European traditions, the creature may be free to roam again. The preferred method of destroying a vampire is by fire. But in the case of the sampiro, staking seems to be an eminently effective option. There is, however, the problem of finding a simpiro's grave, as it is unwise to attack the vampire when it is up and abroad. It is here that tradition offers some clues as to the creature's resting place.

It is said that the grave in which a sampiro is lying is marked by two things. Firstly, it is marked by a faint blue candle-like flame, such as a will-o'-the-wisp. According to legend, such flames appeared, hovering over the graves of robbers, evil men, and magicians at certain times of the year—St. George's Eve (April 22), May Eve (April 30), and Hallowe'en (October 31). St. George's Eve in particular was considered an important time for this, for there was an extremely ancient belief (not only common in Eastern Europe but in the Baltic regions as well) that prior to that date, the earth was poisonous after its long winter frost and would show corruption laid within it around that time. It was therefore inadvisable to sit directly on the ground anywhere near where a suspected sampiro had been laid to rest. Secondly, the soil on the grave itself would be porous and easily disturbed. This is believed to allow air down into the grave and to assist the sampiro to breathe, because it's thought that the creature "sleeps" rather than lies dead. When the grave is detected, the body must be exhumed and laid out for staking with proper prayers and rituals (without the proper rites, the whole procedure is ineffective). The sharpened point of the stake must be placed directly above the heart of the corpse and driven into it with a single blow. If, for any reason, the heart is missed or the stake is not driven in properly, then the sampiro is free to rise again and take its revenge upon the community and, more directly, upon those who have tried to destroy it.

In many parts of Albania, the sampiro has an added menace. Not only does it drink blood from individual victims, but it also, like so many others of its kind, spreads disease and sickness throughout a community. Plagues and epidemics have been put down to the activities of the sampiro, as have high instances of infant mortality in some regions. In some areas, even the very *glance* of a sampiro can induce sickness. From time to time, the creature will move through the countryside, stopping momentarily at the windows of the cottages and houses that it passes. It will gaze in at the people gathered within, and those upon whom its gaze alights will suffer some form of illness (perhaps fatal) very soon after. In this way, whole villages can be affected.

The sampiro is well established in Albanian folklore, and the tales about the creature are numerous across the country. In the Gjere Mountains, for example, near the picturesque town of Gjirokastra, the vampire lore was fairly common.

An old man, not all that well liked by the community, died and was laid to rest in a remote cemetery. About three weeks

after, a mysterious epidemic swept through the mountain area in which he had lived, taking away young children and the elderly—those who were most vulnerable. During the night, several people claimed to have heard the sound of clattering shoes or high heels walking along the road toward the dead man's house, and some of the plague victims claimed to have dreamed about him before they died. This left local people in no doubt that the old man had become a sampiro. This idea was compounded when one of his sons said that he had risen from his bed in the middle of the night to find his father standing in the kitchen of their cottage, wrapped in his grave clothes and with large, staring eyes that were almost hypnotic. The son fled back to bed, and when he returned, the apparition was gone. A priest was called, and he informed the sons that their father indeed must have become one of the Undead and the only way to dispose of the cadaver was to drive a stake into it. Only then would people cease to die and the plague would pass. The dead man's wife and his sons held council with the village elders and they decided to go to the graveyard and carry out the priest's instructions. That evening as they went to the cemetery, just as it was growing dark, several tiny flames seemed to be flickering, like will-o'-the -wisps or marsh gas among the tombstones. This was a sure sign of the presence of more than one sampiro there, and it was judged that each person the creature had killed had become a sampiro in his or her own right. The villagers began to dig into the porous soil of the graves, and the accompanying lights seemed to flicker around the edges more brightly. The first body to be exhumed was that of the old man himself. He was wrapped in his grave cloth, but it was torn and ragged and stained with earth. It was taken that this was what the sampiro wrapped itself in as it walked the roads back to its former home. The corpse itself seemed unusually florid and although it had been in the earth for several weeks, it looked as if it had just been buried. In fact, the old man looked as fresh as when he had been alive. Laying the body out on a slab with many prayers and Christian incantations, as the priest had told them, they drove a hawthorn stake (hawthorn seems to be the prescribed wood for the stake in this case) into its breast. There was a loud and distant cry that did not altogether seem to come from the corpse, and the body seemed to crumble in front of them. Soon it was reduced almost to a skeleton and the horrible stink of corruption filled the air. Just to be on the safe side, the old man's sons and wife had the body burned (an assured way of destroying any vampire) and, from then on, there was no further activity by the sampiro. Miraculously, those who were suffering from the plague and who were still alive began to make a slow recovery back to health. And there were no more sounds at night, suggesting clattering high heels along the roads.

In many cases, the sampiro first attacked its own family or those that it loved, although it often spread disease all across the community. A story from another part of Albania illustrates this point.

A young girl, living near the settlement of Bataris fell deeply in love with a handsome youth who lived close by; and he fell in love with her also. The relationship was, however, questionable because there were suggestions that the young man's mother had dallied with a Turkish soldier, long before he had been born. However, such rumors did not overly concern the lovers. They announced their intention to marry. However, just before the wedding, the boy suffered a terrible accident. Within hours of the catastrophe, he was dead. The girl faced the bereavement with admirable stoicism and, if she wept, she wept in private. An aunt, who lived nearby, fell ill and the maiden seemed to devote most of her time to looking after her. People said that it lifted her mind from her loss. However, there was one drawback—in order to travel to and from

her aunt's house, the girl had to pass the cemetery where her former lover lay and, everyone agreed, it must have been hard for her to do so.

One evening as she was walking home, a slight fog began to rise, just as she approached the burial ground. She passed by the spot and the fog seemed to thicken a little. A little way down the road, she was sure that she heard a sound like high heels on the road behind her but when she turned round, she saw nothing and hurried on home. Shortly afterwards, some livestock—cattle and sheep—in the neighboring villages sickened and died, and there were whispers all through the region that it might be the work of a vampire. This made little impact on the girl, who continued to look after her ailing aunt.

Some nights after the first incident, she passed by the cemetery again and she noticed that the fog was rising once more. Again it thickened, and again she heard the sound like high heels coming after her. This time, however, she stopped. Out of the thickening fog came a terrifying figure, swathed in graveclothes that rose up around its face and two large eyes that stared directly at her and that seemed to glow. It tottered after her on high heels, and as it drew nearer she imagined that she heard something more—her own name whispered by the thing in front of her. With a scream, she turned and ran in the direction of her home, but the sampiro moved quickly and caught her from behind, mouthing her name as it did so. She felt its hot breath on the back of her neck. With another loud yell and an almost superhuman effort, she tore free and ran home. The sampiro ran after her but it was awkward on its heels and she managed to get into her own house and bar the door after her. For many minutes, the creature rattled and whispered outside, but it couldn't get into the cottage. At length, it clattered away, returning to the cemetery. The girl had no doubt in her mind that the sampiro was the revenant of the boy with whom she had once been in love and that he had attacked her because of his great affection for her. This was the way of it

with many sampiros. She informed the elders in her community, and that evening they all made a procession to the cemetery. There, on the grave of the youth, a will-o'-the-wisp was
flickering—a sure sign that he was indeed a sampiro. The body
was exhumed and was found to be very fresh, exhibiting no
signs of decay whatsoever. A stake of yew was brought (it is
interesting to note that the stake is of yew at this time and not
hawthorn, as in the previous story) and was driven into the
corpse's heart with a single blow. Its head was then struck off
and buried separately. The "illnesses" among the cattle and the
sounds on the road ceased immediately after that, and the
youth's corpse was at rest.

The notion of racial difference and of moral rectitude has
an immense significance in the idea of the Albanian vampire,
as does the idea of unusual or exotic sexual practices. Fear of
becoming one of the Undead serves as a powerful social control and often serves to keep the ethnic grouping intact and
free from outside influences.

Although it is certainly a rather fantastic-looking figure,
the sampiro can still instil fear and terror in its victims. When
the moon is bright and there is a suggestion of fog in the air,
the sound of clattering high heels passing along some lonely
road or near some ancient cemetery can bring fear to even the
stoutest heart, for who can say what moves menacingly through
the nighttime Albanian mists?

14.

The Strigoii

ROMANIA

 omania is, of course, the traditional home of the vampire because it incorporates the province of Transylvania, where the most famous of all vampire tales—*Dracula*—is set. Images of ruined castles, and sets of lofty, mist-swathed East European crags; of deep dark forests, filled with wolves and all manner of unspeakable horrors; or of cape-shrouded Magyar noblemen slipping through the darkness have long dominated vampire lore. Indeed, it is hard to think of vampires *without* associating them with Romanian nobility. The reality is, of course, much different.

As in many other cultures, the notion of the returning dead in Romanian folklore is a strong one. Those who have lived evil lives or who had committed dark sins, such as witchcraft, were not admitted to Paradise, but were condemned to wander the world forever. And, during their lifetimes, they

might be similarly cursed. For example, those who secretly practiced the dark arts might be subject to unnatural lusts and desires. These may include a lust for blood—usually animal blood. These are the *moroii*, or *moroaica*, witches and warlocks of rural Romania who often subsist upon blood. Although they are classified as "living vampires," the term is usually taken to mean a witch or sorcerer of the blackest kind—a person who has deliberately sold his or her soul to the Evil One in return for worldly power and influence (usually at a local level). They are particularly easy to spot, as the males are exceptionally pale and are almost hairless. (The figure of the vampire played by Maximillian Schreck in F.W. Murnau's 1922 film, *Nosferatu*, could be taken to be loosely based on the Romanian moroii.) Female moroii, by contrast, are extremely red-faced and have full, red lips. It is widely believed that the moroii can assume any animal shape they choose—a bird or a moth being the most common. In this guise they can

travel throughout the countryside, doing harm to their neighbors. They also had the power to send their spirits out, invisibly, as their bodies slept in order to create mischief and disasters in the area, to spread disease, and to attack people as they slumbered. However, they were, themselves, subject to all the ailments that befell ordinary humans and they could be killed, although to do so ran the risk of turning them into something far worse.

All manner of people could become moroii, and it could be through the simplest of causes: those who neglected Mass, those who stole, those who lied, and those who practiced witchcraft. Those who lusted after their neighbors' wives and the illegitimate children of priests were especially susceptible. Those whose mothers had neglected holy rites whilst pregnant were also at risk, as were those upon whom a vampire had looked whilst they were in the womb. Those who had eaten uncooked meat or who had drunk impure homemade spirits also ran the risk of becoming moroii. Those who had accidentally swallowed a bee or a fly might become one, too, because the insect might be a witch or wizard in another guise. Those whose mothers had eaten unleavened bread or who had looked with lust on a foreigner might later become a witch. Similarly, those who were left-handed were deemed to be attracted to the black arts. The list was almost endless.

Traits of the Strigoii

Because they were living—and, for all intents and purposes, human—such moroii could die from natural causes or else be killed. This would turn them into *strigoii*, an even worse and even more deadly creature. Strigoii were the walking dead—physical corpses that knew no rest and were motivated solely by evil. All humanity appeared to have left them and they were now the implacable enemies of humankind. The name has its origins in the ancient Roman *striges*, or witches.

These were individuals (usually living) who went about at night in the form of birds (sometimes half human and half bird), spreading filth and disease amongst the Latin communities. They were also credited with having evil supernatural powers, which they used against Roman society. This translated into the walking dead of Romania. It was inevitable that a member of the moroii would, after death, become a strigoii, but sometimes a deceased corpse could become one in its own right. The corpse might become one of the strigoii and could return to haunt the living if a shadow fell across an open coffin; if a bird or animal passed over the body; if it wasn't buried with proper rites; if the person involved was a suicide; and if a creature walked over the grave.

The strigoii *might* drink blood but more often they ate normal food (as did the moroii). However, rather than drinking either blood or vital fluids, they could draw the energies from a person by a kind of osmosis, leaving them weak, sickly, and helpless. Besides attacking people, the strigoii spread disease from house to house, leaving death and desolation in their wakes. They also had the ability (usually invisibly) to engage in poltergeist-like activities, pulling crockery from dressers or making coals suddenly start out of the fire. Only as a last resort did they drink blood and then only from their families or from people whom they knew (that is, within their own community).

When they moved about, strigoii were easily spotted. They moved slowly, as if they were sleepwalkers, and though their right eye was closed, their left eye was always open and was blood-red in color. They exhibited a florid complexion and often grew reddish hair. When in the grave, their bodies remained uncorrupted, and their hair and nails continued to grow. At times, the creature may well have become bloated and swollen with blood.

Protection Against the Strigoii

There were ways of locating the tomb or grave of a strigoii. In the rural countryside, such graves were said to be marked by a blue flame, like that of a candle, which burned a little way above the ground under which the strigoii lay. These burned quite brightly at night and could be seen from a distance away. Another method was to take a 7-year-old male child, dress him in white, set him astride a white horse, and turn the animal loose in a churchyard. Wherever the horse stopped, there the vampire lay. This latter method was often used by communities that felt themselves persecuted by the Undead.

It was further believed that, in order to breathe in the grave, the vampires made small holes to the surface in order to admit air. If small holes or cavities were found on a grave, then that was where a vampire lay. The body would then be exhumed and inspected by the local priest. If it was found to be uncorrupted or bloated in any way (although it might have been bloated with gasses, it was taken that it was swollen with blood), it was adjudged to be a vampire. The priest would then say prayers over it, and the heart would be cut from it and burned. In some cases, the head might also be struck off using the blade of a gravedigger's shovel and the mouth filled with herbs (though not necessarily garlic). Unlike many other vampires in neighboring areas of the world, Romanian strigoii *could* be affected by strong sunlight, especially the first rays of the morning. To avoid these, the creature had to be back in its grave by sunrise.

It was widely believed throughout Eastern Europe that strigoii were particularly obsessive entities. In certain localities, stratagems were devised to keep the creature occupied and away from potential victims until the sun rose and it had to return to the tomb. Poppy seeds, for example, might be scattered around the grave of a suspected vampire—the notion being that, as it emerged from the earth, the being would notice

these and attempt to gather them up. This would keep it busy throughout the night. (Something similar may have been used to delay the Irish vampire Abhartach, by scattering thorns all around the gravesite). Other diversions included scattering flower petals or clothes to delay the strigoii in its activities, and so save its victims.

Wine was also said to drive away the Undead. Potential victims should therefore, it was said, consume large quantities in case they should be attacked. Wine, especially cheap wine, tainted the blood and so made it unpalatable to the strigoii. Even the smallest amount—no more than a glass—would work. Onions too, whether raw or fried, were abhorrent to the vampire, and it would avoid anyone who even smelt of them. Certain herbs might also be used as well, although there is no specific mention of garlic.

Vlad Tepes

In most vampire legends from this part of the world, the vampires are all common people and there seems to be little or no mention of the aristocracy. Some folklorists claim, however, that Romanian vampires trace their origins back to Vlad Tepes, a brutal ruler of the province of Wallachia and a stout defender of Christianity against Turkish incursion. Although classed as a "ruler," Vlad II (c. 1431–1476) was probably little more than a localized warlord, holding onto his Wallachian dominions. His father, Vlad I, had been accorded the sobriquet "Dracul" (Dragon) by the Holy Roman Emperor because of his stalwart and ferocious defense against Turkish incursions, and so his son took the title "Dracula" (Little Dragon). He maintained a "court," which received ambassadors, and there seems little doubt that he was a skilled and competent politician—well able to play Turks and Christians against each other. (He was extremely conversant with Turkish ways, having been held under house arrest as a Turkish prisoner together with his brother Radu during his father's reign.) There is also little doubt that he was a tyrant and an incredibly cruel man who was also known as "Vlad the Impaler," due to the fact that he placed the bodies of captured enemies at the top of high, pointed stakes, allowing the weight of their bodies and the force of gravity to carry them earthwards and impale them. Legend says that he gave great banquets where he and his guests could watch these unfortunates as they were impaled. When he allegedly received some Turkish ambassadors to his court, the men refused to remove their fezzes, whereupon Dracula had the hats nailed to their foreheads. Although he was undoubtedly barbaric and cruel, there is no account of him actually drinking blood. The legend pertaining to the drinking of blood perhaps predates the tyrant. Yet it was the warlord Dracula whom the Irish writer Bram Stoker chose as the template for the most famous of all vampire creations: the bloodthirsty Transylvanian count.

Stoker's novel had much more to do with the problems and perceptions of late-19th-century Ireland and England than it had with Eastern Europe. The cape-swathed count reflected the view of an emerging working class of the aristocracy (the other "monster" from that period is Jack the Ripper, whose figure also reflected aristocratic values): the "native soil" in which the vampire had to lie hinted at land issues between the English and the Irish, and the female figures in the novel mirrored the confusion concerning an emerging feminism. Stoker had never been to Eastern Europe and so he used tales from his friends and travel writers. He may also have used ancient Irish legends from Celtic sources. His book was enough to firmly locate the vampire in Eastern Europe, and there well have been at least some historical reason for doing so, for, although vampires exist in almost every culture, they seem to have adopted a particularly prominent role there.

Vampire Epidemic

In the early-to-mid 1700s, many provinces in Eastern Europe experienced what might be described as a "vampire epidemic." Given the geographical context, this was not unusual—other areas such as Germany and Austria experienced similar "epidemics" around the same time—but it was enough to seriously alarm the Christian authorities there and also at the Vatican. Already the Church was taking an interest in vampirism (there had been small "waves" of vampire hysteria in Eastern Germany) and learned theological scholars were turning their minds to the matter. Did vampires actually exist? And, if so, what were they? Did their powers come from the devil? Vampires were becoming a fairly vexed question for the Church.

Peter Plogojowitz

Two cases in particular had achieved some notoriety. Both of them concerned what were taken by local people to reflect the belief in moroii. The first, in 1725, concerned a certain Peter Plogojowitz, an inhabitant of the village of Kislova in the Rahm district of Austrian-occupied Serbia. Having lived a seemingly unexceptional life, Plogojowitz died at the age of 62. Three days after he was interred, he appeared again at his own house, explaining to his startled son that he was hungry and asking for something to eat. He was given some food, which he ate, and then he left. This was not the end, however, for two evenings later he returned with the same demands. This time, his son refused him, and although the corpse went away, Plogojowitz Junior was found dead in bed the next morning. Shortly after, several villagers in the vicinity of his house took ill with exhaustion and died from allegedly severe blood loss.

In all, nine or 10 people, including women and children, died in this way. Before they died, some of the victims recounted a remarkable dream in which they claimed that the

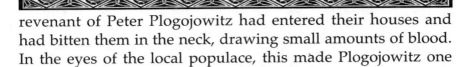

revenant of Peter Plogojowitz had entered their houses and had bitten them in the neck, drawing small amounts of blood. In the eyes of the local populace, this made Plogojowitz one of the strigoii—the malicious dead.

In light of these deaths and the allegations, a local magistrate filed a report with the Imperial Provisor, Gradask District, commander of the Imperial forces, who immediately responded with a personal visit to the village. On his orders, the graves of the recently dead, including that of Peter Plogojowitz, were opened and their contents examined. The body of Plogojowitz was found to be flushed, as if suffused with blood; the eyes were open; and it appeared as if it was breathing very gently. The hair and nails appeared to have grown whilst in the tomb and several minor wounds that he had exhibited before death appeared to have healed. Significantly, the edges of the mouth were smeared with what looked to be fresh blood. The other corpses were already in a state of decay and not one showed similar manifestations. The Provisor concluded that Plogojowitz was indeed a vampire and that the corpse manifested some form of diabolical life. Subsequently, he summoned an executioner to Kislova and instructed him to drive a wooden stake through the body. As the stake entered, fresh blood gushed from all the main orifices, and the body sank in on itself. The body was then burned. The others were reburied, but in order to protect them, a number of herbs, including garlic and whitethorn, were placed in their coffins.

The story became widespread, largely due to the writings of the Marquis d' Argens, who took a serious interest in more unusual matters and recorded it in his *Lettres Julives*, which enjoyed a wide circulation amongst the intelligentsia of the time, being translated into English in 1729. This ensured that the Plogojowitz story became something of a legend.

Arnold Paole

Two years later, in 1727, another, even more celebrated case occurred, once again in the East of Europe. This involved a former soldier named Arnold Paole, from the village of Medvegia, north of Belgrade. Paole had been born in Medvegia but had gone off to join the Austrian army, serving in a part of Greece or "Turkish Serbia," before coming home again in the spring of 1727 to work as a farm laborer. By all accounts, he was quite a handsome, good-natured, and honest man. He was actively pursued by several young local women before becoming engaged to one of them and planning to settle down. However, there was a story about him that he himself had recounted. It stemmed from his army days. Whilst on duty at a fort in Turkish Serbia, he had been attacked by what he believed to have been one of the strigoii and had been badly bitten. According to his story, he had hunted down and killed the vampire, although this may have simply been embellishment. The tale gave him a certain amount of status in the community but it also tinged him with an air of mystery and danger.

Shortly after his engagement, Paole suffered a severe fall from a hay-wagon and cracked his head on the surface of a country road. The accident was a fatal one and, though he lingered for several days, Paole finally succumbed and died. His body was buried almost immediately.

Some weeks after his burial, strange reports began to circulate around Medvegia that Paole had been seen in several locations close by. Given the story that he'd claimed to have been attacked by a vampire, panic began to spread through the region and people called upon community leaders to determine whether the appearance might be a vampire. Forty days after he was buried, the grave of Arnold Paole was opened. This was done in the presence of two military surgeons, who assisted in lifting the lid from the coffin. To their surprise, they found that the corpse was extremely fresh, as if

Paole had just died, with what seemed to be a growth of new skin under an outer layer of that which was dead and decaying. Nails and hair also seemed to have continued to grow. There was no explanation for this, and the cadaver was declared a vampire. The body was staked and, according to legend, emitted a loud groan and issued a vast amount of blood. The head was severed and the entire body burned. It was expected that this was the end of the matter, and for several years it was.

In 1731, in the same area, a number of people were experiencing intense exhaustion, stemming, it was thought, from loss of blood. Several of them died and, once again, rumors of vampirism began to circulate. Surgeons were once more summoned from Belgrade. They inspected some of the dead bodies, including that of a 10-year-old girl named Stenko, who displayed "unmistakable" traces of vampirism. Whilst the examinations were underway, another victim died—this time a man named Milo. Popular rumor said that he had been attacked by the revenant of Arnold Paole. The surgeons reported back, and word of their findings reached Vienna and the court of the Austrian Emperor, who ordered an enquiry to be conducted by Regimental Field Sergeant Johannes Fluckinger.

Fluckinger was appointed in December 1731, and he immediately headed for Medvegia to take charge of an Imperial investigation. On his orders, Milo's body was exhumed and was discovered to be in a similar condition to that of Arnold Paole back in 1727. Was it possible that the soldier's revenant had returned? Fluckinger's inquiry reached the conclusion that Paole had vampirized several cows before his body had been committed to ashes. Those cows had in turn vampirized other beasts over the years, and the dead had feasted on the flesh of those tainted animals. The bodies of all those who had died within the last two or three months were then dug up—a massive and grisly undertaking for the small community. Forty cadavers were disinterred, of which 17 were found to be in the

same state as Paole's body. Each one of them was staked and burned.

Because of the involvement of the authorities, the case was very well documented, and the report, which Fluckinger presented to the Austrian Emperor in 1732, was widely circulated. By the summer and autumn of that year, extracts from it had been published in periodicals in both France and England, as well as several extremely selective accounts of the Medvegia vampires. This notoriety was enough to make Arnold Paole one of the most famous "vampires" of his day, and raised discussion about the nature of the creatures (particularly concerning East European strigoii) amongst many European intellectuals.

If vampires were of interest to secular people, they were equally so to the Church. Certain theologians began to show an interest in the phenomenon from a religious perspective— whether the dead could actually return, whether they attacked the living, and, if so, under what circumstances.

Giuseppe Davanzati

One of the earliest theologians to consider the vampire problem and to write about it was the Italian academic Giuseppe Davanzati (1665–1755), the archbishop of Travi and patriarch of Alexandria. An elderly man and a respected scholar, Davanzati's period as archbishop in 1745 coincided with waves of vampirism in various parts of Europe. Discussions on the problem were initiated by Cardinal Schtrattembach, the bishop of Olmutz in Germany, which appeared to be experiencing the worst of these plagues. In 1738 the bishop asked Davanzatti for his comments and made available to him a number of reports, including one on Arnold Paole. Davanzati did not publish his report (*Disserttazione sopra I Vampiri*) until 1744, after "much considered thought and research."

He concluded that vampires (strigoii) did not exist but were the result of fevered human imagination. The vampire "epidemics" that swept parts of Eastern Europe (especially the part we now know as Romania) were the result of hysteria and fantasies amongst an illiterate and credulous peasantry. Such notions, warned Davanzati, were not to be countenanced by sophisticated and educated men. His thesis generated widespread interest, and the archbishop emerged as a leading authority on vampires both within the Church and the secular spheres, with his work being reprinted in 1789. However, it was to be overshadowed by the work of another French theologian, Dom Antoine Augustin Calmet (1672–1757), who reached rather different conclusions.

Dom Antoine Augustin Calmet

Like Davanzati, Calmet was a respected Churchman and a celebrated biblical scholar. A Benedictine, he had taught philosophy in the Abbey at Moyen-Moutier and was extremely well known in the European scholarly community for his works of biblical criticism. As a scholar, he was well aware of the detailed accounts of strigoii coming out of Eastern Europe and was intrigued by accounts of the blood-sucking dead creatures. Two years after Davanzati had published his essay dismissing vampires as a figment of hysterical imagination (1746), Calmet also brought out a publication based on reports from Eastern Europe: *Dissertations sur les Apparitions des Anges des Demons et les Espirits, et sur les revenants et Vampires de Hungrie, de Boheme, de Moravie et de Silesie.* Calmet had read most of the interviews with people in parts of Eastern Europe concerning the strigoii and was impressed with them. He thought it unreasonable to dismiss them completely out of hand as Davanzati had done. Besides, such walking dead would have theological implications for the belief in an afterlife. The Church, however, seemed to side with Davanzati and, through

the Paris Sourbonne, it roundly condemned the reports upon which Calmet had based his conclusions. In reply, Calmet also condemned the hysteria that had surrounded some of the reported incidents of vampirism and the exhumation of dead bodies, as well as certain aspects of rural folklore, but he seemed to suggest that vampires *might* conceivably exist. He was immediately attacked by his colleagues as being credulous and gullible. Perhaps due to the controversy, Calmet's book became a best-seller and did much to bring the concept of the East European strigoii to wider attention.

Calmet was ultimately unable to conclude that the reports supported the contention of his rivals that such phenomena were due to natural causes, but he declined to propose any alternative. Whilst he did not openly state that the strigoii existed, the main thrust of his work seemed to lie in that direction. Interest in his book swelled even more: the volume was reprinted in French editions in 1746, 1747, and 1748. German and English editions appeared in 1752 and 1759, respectively, and it was reprinted in English in 1850 under the title *The Phantom World*. As it reached more and more people, it generated more and more controversy. In 1755 and 1756, the Austrian Empress Maria Theresa (herself a noted and formidable sceptic) issued laws designed to stop the spread of vampire hysteria. These included edicts that removed all reports on alleged vampirism from the hands of the clergy and placed them under civil jurisdiction. This legislation came into effect one year before Calmet's death. The waves of hysteria and the debates that they generated served to place Eastern Europe at the very centre of vampire belief, and it was probably this notion upon which Stoker fastened when he came to write *Dracula*.

The Vampire-Hunter

One other aspect deserves mention and it is also a concept that Stoker used in his novel and has further been used in novels and films right up to the present day. This is the idea of the vampire-hunter—as in the Dutch occult specialist Abraham Van Helsing. This, too, has its origins amongst the strigoii of Eastern Europe. In folklore, particularly amongst East European gypsies, it was believed that for everyone born who would ultimately become a strigoii, someone was also born with the power to slay it,, and, in this way, God kept control over the dead. It is thought that in some parts of Romania, vampire-hunters travelled among the villages, apparently hunting down the Undead in the manner of witch-hunters in early modern England. They would enter a village in which there was widespread sickness and ascribe this to the work of vampires. They would then begin to exhume a number of bodies to inspect them, creating hysteria and unrest in the locality and distress to the families concerned. This activity was viewed both with displeasure and alarm by the civil authorities and was probably the imperative behind the empress's edict.

All these folkloric factors may well have influenced Stoker's choice of setting for his vampire novel, and they have certainly made Romania (of which Transylvania is a part) a kind of "vampire capital" of the world. Today, vampirism is inextricably linked with Eastern Europe in general and Romania in particular, and visions of a caped Balkan count epitomize the entire belief. The truth may be rather different and may not lie in near-ruined castles or forgotten fortresses, but rather in the wandering moroii and strogoii of the Romanian villages. Although we cannot say for certain that such vampires exist, perhaps Calmet was right not to dismiss them completely.

15.

The Tikoloshe

SOUTH AFRICA

Although many vampiric entities are scattered across the African continent, as with many other cultures, confusion exists as to whether they are actually the walking dead or those possessed by demons. The diverse indigenous cultures that comprise the African nation (both North and South) coupled with the imported beliefs of the Colonial powers have led to a rich panoply of evil entities and forces that can threaten everyday life. As elsewhere in the world, a further consideration is given as to whether the hostile dead (and vampires in particular) are linked with and controlled by witchcraft.

The Tikoloshe and Witchcraft

In the delta country of the Niger River, for instance, it is believed that witches regularly gather in order to work harm against their neighbors. In such conclave, they can draw the blood and internal organs from anyone they wish by using magic. Alternatively, if a witch can obtain a specimen of a prospective victim's excrement, he or she can use it to draw the vitality from that person, leaving them a pale and withered husk. To this end, the effects of diseases such as tuberculosis are put down to malefic and vampiric witchcraft. Indeed, in Nigeria, the main type of vampire is an *obeyifo*, who is a living person dwelling in the local community who uses his or her vampire powers against neighbors. Confusingly, the obeyifo is also a name used amongst Gold Coast tribes to describe a shapeshifting wizard who flies around in various guises (a bird, a fly, and so on), drinking blood and semen. Amongst the Ashanti peoples of Ghana, however, the *asasbonsam* are witches who live deep in the jungle in tall trees to wait for travellers to pass beneath them. They do not have ordinary feet, but instead have large hooks with which they can carry their victims aloft and "store" them amongst the high branches. When required, blood can be drawn from the victim's thumb to sustain the vampire. The Yoko people of Nigeria further believe that disembodied witches (sometimes travelling as spheres of burning light) could draw the heart and liver from sleeping victims, or that witches, perched on the roof of a house, could draw up and devour the heart of an individual, simply by magic.

The Ewe people of Southern Togo greatly feared the *adze*, a vampire that often assumed the shape of a firefly. If caught, this being might revert to a quasi-human form—that of a small humanoid figure, hunchbacked with sharp talons and jet-black skin—in which guise it is at its most dangerous. Then it could kill its victim, drink his blood, and eat his heart and liver before it was sated. Many of these witches were invariably male

and were also rather old. However, the *impundulu* of the tribes of the Southern Cape was always female. In fact, the "curse" of the vampire was usually passed genetically from mother to daughter and could not be removed from a female line. This creature was also strongly associated with witchcraft, and the impundulu was usually considered to be the servant of a witch or witch doctor, and was bound to carry out his or her orders. It is used to attack and debilitate the magician's enemies or to steal things from their houses. The impundulu, however, had an insatiable appetite, mainly for blood, and had to be fed almost continuously—sometimes using the magician's own blood, sometimes the blood of its victims.

Traits of the Tikoloshe

Arguably the most celebrated of these vampiric servants and sorcerous familiars is the *tikoloshe*, or *tokoloshe*, a creature of the Xhosa people of Lisotho and the southernmost African plains. Like many other such entities in Africa, the being is a mixture of vampire and demon, and has strong associations with magicians and witches. In many of the Xhosa legends, the tikoloshe is a demon that is often connected with water and physically resembles a baboon. Short, stocky, and hirsute, and often with a high, balding forehead, it goes about either at night or in daylight, swinging its long arms like a monkey. However, it has many powers and, as many African devil-creatures, it can change its shape when it suits. It can, for example, appear as an ordinary human being, although it may still bear some monkey-like characteristics. It can also take the guise of a great black bird-like being with a skull head, soaring over the villages and seeking out victims. The tikoloshe is male and is widely known for its voracious sexual appetite. Therefore, most of its victims tend to be local village women. The entity does not actually feed on blood as such, but rather on the energies of those whom it ravishes, leaving them weak

and tired. Too frequent attention by the creature can also result in death from exhaustion. The tikoloshe will also travel many miles to attack a victim. There are stories of them seeking out women with whom they can copulate in Natal and Johannesburg.

The being will often approach a village woman at any hour of the day in a human disguise. It will greet her in a very friendly (perhaps overly familiar) way, offering to carry heavy bundles of sticks or clothes for her or maybe her water jar in return for sexual favors. If she refuses, it will revert to its natural horrific form and leap upon her almost before she knows it—the tikoloshe can move with incredible speed—and proceed to ravish her. Tikoloshe can also turn up, in human form, at communal dances, appearing as attractive neighbors who are dressed very grandly. At social occasions, they will be very polite, charming, and seductive, and their words are so beguiling that many of the village women to whom they talk quickly fall under their spell and are lured away into the forest. If a woman does not succumb to its charms, the tikoloshe will invariably revert to its original form and take her by force.

Like many other such creatures, the tikoloshe can be used by a sorcerer against his or her enemies. Such liaisons are usually the result of some form of agreement between the witch and the creature itself. In return for aiding a female witch, the tikoloshe will demand milk from her cows, food, and lodging, as well as the right to have sex with her whenever he pleases. From a male sorcerer, it can demand meat, milk, and women with whom to copulate as the mood takes it. In return, it is obliged to carry out the witch or sorcerer's evil demands. It sometimes does its work in the shape of a great skull-headed bird with filth dripping from its claws, spreading disease and plague everywhere it goes. In this guide it is also called a *hili*. The mere touch of the thing's claws can create a lingering sickness that even the most powerful magic can barely dispel.

The Mantindane

A form of tikoloshe is also found amongst the Bantu peoples of Kenya, only here it is also known as "the dwarf." Sometimes referred to as a tikoloshe and at other times as a *mantindane* (fairy man), it has the height of a 2-year-old child but with a wide and stocky body. It is covered in an ochre-colored fur, with long reddish hair hanging low over its forehead. It has a small orange-colored moustache and hair on its feet and on the backs of its hands—but none on the palms or on the soles. Its pointed ears are pressed back against its narrow skull and it sports a penis that looks more like a long tail. Its eyes are narrow, slitted, dark, and wicked. It wears no clothes and lives in caves and burrows along a riverbank or in the river itself. It subsists on the blood of the Bantu people's cattle. The Bantu believe that this is a wild creature that is not

wholly evil in itself. However, it can be easily manipulated by dark magic and witchcraft. Once enslaved by magical means, the tikoloshe can then be sent out on evil errands, such as causing harm to the magician's neighbors. To do this, it invokes one of its special powers: the ability to render itself invisible. In this state, it can carry poisons into a house, which it then secretes somewhere so that foul fumes will infect those who live there. It may also carry a buck's horn, filled with foul mixtures that have been prepared by the magician, and hide it along the river where drinking pots are filled. This produces sickness and disease in a community, and its attentions may even result in death. Even when a person is eating, a tikoloshe may approach him, invisibly, and drop a small amount of poison on his spoon. Afterwards, the creature will draw blood from the individual's cattle and in this way it is rewarded for carrying out its evil master's bidding.

Capturing a Tikoloshe

Many of the Bantu people believe that there are ways to catch a tikoloshe. Some tribes believe that the creature has an insatiable craving for blood and fresh milk, both of which it will drink straight from the cow. In order to confuse the farmers, they will frequently drive all the cattle into the kraal so the owners think the cows they have been fighting and have drawn blood, or that the calves have drunk all the milk. In order to imprison the tikoloshe, farmers will often employ the services of a local witch-doctor or herbalist. The tikoloshe will always enter the kraal at the same place—usually from the rear of the enclosure. It is here that the magician sets his magical traps. He draws an enchanted circle on a spot where he knows that the dwarf will walk and sprinkles it with magic herbal powder. Then a cow is placed in a convenient position where the tikoloshe will approach it to drink its blood or milk. If the dwarf steps onto the enchanted circle, it is paralyzed and cannot move, and its powers of invisibility will be destroyed forever. Although he is now a prisoner, he will be freed if someone points to it and exclaims, "Look! A tikoloshe!" At this point, the creature will vanish and is free to take its revenge and terrorize the community once more. In this instance, it will be twice as disruptive and violent as before. It is therefore important that the magician or herbalist be the one who captures the being. If he does this, then he can use the immobilized tikoloshe in his own preparations. It is ground up—fat, bone, and sinew—and turned into a strong medicine, which can be used to catch others of its kind. This service is usually carried out for a fee by local herbalists, and so a captured tikoloshe is of great financial value to any magician.

Amongst the Xhosa people, however, there is no such tradition of capturing a tikoloshe, and avoidance is often better than a cure. Because the tikoloshe is so small and because it attacks only sleepers, it is thought prudent to raise the height of the bed. Therefore, a sleeping palate, especially that on which a female sleeps, is raised on stacks of bricks. In this way, the sleeper might be able to escape the attentions of the short tikoloshe. A sleeper may also rest with an iron knife across his or her breast, as this will also dissuade the creature. In Swaziland, children are considered to be extremely at risk and it's thought that the tikoloshe will carry them away to a burrow along the riverbank, where it will drink their blood.

There are many tales about the tikoloshe all over southern Africa.

One evening a man was returning to his hut when he was horrified to see what looked like a tikoloshe on its way out. He said nothing to his wife, but the next night he pretended to go out again. This time, however, he waited a little way from the hut to see what would happen. As soon as the sun started to go down, the tikoloshe returned. The man entered the hut and, to his dismay, he saw his wife copulating with the hairy intruder.

As it did so, the thing was drawing all the good from her and was turning her into a withered skeleton. In a fit of fury, he killed the tikoloshe but he couldn't bring himself to kill the woman who had copulated with it, even though he suspected that she might be "tainted" by it. He tied up the creature's body and paraded it through the village, holding it high above him to show others what had been in his house. Later he went to see an herbalist, an expert in these matters (known as a tikoloshe or tokoloshe man), and asked him to come and cleanse his house with burning herbs and incantations. The expert told him that he would have to send his wife away and have nothing more to do with her, as she had been corrupted by a tikoloshe and was now no use to him. This the man gratefully did, as his wife was not the vibrant woman that he had married but appeared old and wasted after her encounter. The other villagers understood, so they returned his wife's dowry of cattle to him and, sadly, he returned to his lonely hut. He did not take another wife and many of the husbands in the village knew that there were other tikoloshe living nearby along the river and that perhaps their own wives would one day be in danger from them. The tikoloshe man in their village was never really idle.

Indeed, the tikoloshe or tokoloshe may arguably be one of the very few vampiric creatures that has had a pop song written about it. In 1971, John Kongos reached number four in the UK charts with a record called *Tokoloshe Man* (a reference to the herbal practitioners and magicians who could deal with the creature). Kongos, who had been born in Johannesburg, may well have known what he was singing about because in the late 1950s / early 1960s, the shantytown of the outlying suburbs were believed to have experienced a minor infestation of the entities, many of them acting invisibly, of course.

So as night falls over southern Africa, and the lights go on in the shanty districts and fires are lit in rural huts, perhaps it is wise to cast a glance out into the gathering dusk. All sorts of strange and supernatural entities may be coming and going out there—especially the tikoloshe.

16.

Vampire Ladies

UNITED STATES OF AMERICA

If there were a "vampire capital" of America, where would it be? San Francisco? New York? At least that's what the modern films tell us. But what if it were to be a small hamlet in rural Rhode Island? What if one of the smallest states in the Union was to have a vampire tradition that stretched back over several hundred years?

Nelly Vaughan

In a remote and overgrown cemetery near the village of Coventry, Rhode Island, there once stood a worn headstone bearing a singular, almost chilling inscription: "I am waiting

and watching for you." The marker, which marked the last resting place of Nelly Vaughan, who died in 1889 at the age of 19, is now long gone, but the legacy of Rhode Island's "vampire ladies" (of which she is said to have been one) lives on along the narrow roads and shady woods of the dreaming countryside.

Even in 1889, when Nelly Vaughan was interred, the notion of vampires was not new in America. In fact, the tradition stretched back to times when the first white settlers had made their homes on the eastern side of the continent. Writing in the late 17th century, the Reverend Deodat Lawson, minister at the now-infamous Salem Village (part of the Massachusetts Bay Colony) and author of the first printed account of the Salem Witch Trials, gives one of the first accounts of a vampiric attack. He was staying at the house of Nathaniel Ingersoll, when Mary Walcott, one of the "afflicted girls" (one of those who had allegedly been the subject of witchcraft), came to see him. Whilst standing near the door, she suddenly experienced a "bite" on her wrist, as if to draw blood, and by the light of a candle the minister glimpsed a mark on the flesh there. It may, of course, have been no more than the bite from a large insect, but the demonologist Montague Summers (claiming access to other papers) remarks that the girl experienced a prolonged loss of energy afterwards—as if it had been drained from her.

During the 1890s, great speculation concerning vampire activity centered on a house on Green Street in Schenectady, New York. An odd humanoid silhouette, formed out of fungus and mold, had appeared upon the cellar floor. No amount of sweeping or scrubbing could remove the outline, which seemed to generate a musty smell and an unmistakeable coldness. The figure appeared to be that of a reclining man, and its very presence in the gloomy cellar generated a feeling of unease and even fear amongst the inhabitants of the house above. It was later discovered that the building had been raised on the site of an old Dutch burying ground (when the city was a Dutch colony known as New Amsterdam) where several ne'er-do-wells and magicians had been buried during the governorship of Peter Stuyvesant. One theory suggested that the outline was a vampire trying to leave its grave. This idea seemed borne out by the fact that several of those living in the building often felt unaccountably weak, as if their vital energies were being drained away. It was prevented from assuming full demonic shape, so the legend said, because of "a virtuous spell" that had been placed on the ground. It was allegedly still there when the house was eventually demolished. The story was, however, widely reported and almost certainly seems to have inspired the famous American horror writer H.P. Lovecraft in his story *The Shunned House*, in which a sinister outline also appears on a cellar floor.

But it was in Rhode Island and in some of the surrounding states that the belief in vampires was to take a stronger and more persistent root. The rural landscape of New England is idyllic—particularly as winter approaches. Time seems to stand still in some places—twisting little roads lead off through the woods to some secret, whitewashed house tucked away in a hollow; the trees wave in the faintest breeze as though seething with some inner life; and in Rhode Island, the air is heavy with the pungent scents of woodsmoke and apples. It is still not difficult to imagine that one has been transported back to some former, less complicated time.

But as the winter gloom sets in, Rhode Island sometimes shows a darker, more sinister side. A significant part of the history of the state has been written in Revolutionary blood, and these quiet woodlands have often sheltered both Colonial troops and British Redcoats that raked the narrow roads with musket fire. The old Colonial houses, sometimes abandoned and given over to mold and decay, are hidden away in shady hollows and at the end of dirt lanes. Numerous tiny

cemeteries, overgrown and ringed with encroaching foliage, dot the back roads leading between the various villages and hamlets. In such a countryside, even today, it's easy to see how the slumbering dead that lie in these graveyards might somehow rise and attack the living.

Coupled with this suggestion, during the hundred years that lay between the respective ends of the 18th and 19th centuries, another spectre arose: the spectre of disease. Epidemics amongst the communities, such as the great consumption (tuberculosis) outbreaks in Connecticut, Massachusetts, Vermont, and Rhode Island during the late 1800s, caused people to fail and waste away, almost inexplicably. The symptoms of the disease corresponded to the results of vampiric activity—loss of strength and appetite; the coughing up of blood, which remained around the edges of the mouth; a marble-like pallor; and the sensation of a weight on the chest as one lay in bed.

Allied to this overall impression were the often peculiar religious practices and beliefs of various fundamentalist sects throughout the region. These were groups such as Shadrack Ireland's "Brethren of the New Light" (part of the so-called New England "New Light Stir") whose uncoffined dead lay in vast underground stone chambers beneath the rural hillsides awaiting the Great Day of Judgement. All these elements combined to form the basis of a vampire belief throughout Rhode Island that lasted slightly more than 100 years and manifested itself in the legend of a series of "vampire ladies," which haunted the nightmares of people across the state.

Sarah Tillinghast

Though there are many variations of the legend, the first of these "ladies" is usually named as Sarah Tillinghast, who died in South County in the year 1796. Her father, Stukley Tillinghast (nicknamed "Snuffy" because of his dull, snuff-colored clothes),

was a well-known apple farmer in the region (he had also been a former captain in the local militia during the Colonial Wars) and her family was reasonably well-off.

Throughout the Colonial Wars, he and his wife, Honour, managed to marry and raise a large family which, by 1798, numbered eight daughters and six sons—the youngest arriving in October of that year. With the approaching winter, however, Snuffy began to experience strange dreams in which he was walking through his orchards noting that half the fruit on the branches was rotten. Through the autumnal mists he heard his daughter, Sarah, calling to him in a low, insistent voice, although he couldn't see her anywhere between the trees. Troubled by the nightmare, he first sought the advice of the local pastor, Benjamin Northup, who advised him to pray and read his Bible. South County—indeed, much of Rhode Island—was in a continual state of unease at the time. The Revolutionary War had just concluded, and many Americans feared an attempt by Britain to retake her former colonies by invasion. There were thought to be a number of British sympathizers living in Rhode Island with the purpose of undermining the state in advance of an invasion from England. Everything was viewed with suspicion. And on top of this, diseases came and went. (Many suspected that these were nothing more than the poisoning of wells by British agents.) Snuffy tried to put the dream to the back of his mind, but his family was about to be hit by a terrible tragedy.

Sarah, then age 19, had always been a dreamy girl, given to wandering amongst the small graveyards where the recently buried Revolutionary soldiers lay. From time to time, she would take books of poetry there to read, seating herself on some grave-slab. Her father indulged her and excused her work about the farm, for without a doubt, Sarah was his favorite. However, on returning from a walk to a churchyard one evening, she professed herself ill and took to her bed. Soon

she was in the grip of a raging fever, which, despite her mother's ministrations, wouldn't leave her. Within a matter of weeks, she was dead. The doctor's diagnosis was consumption.

Several more weeks passed whilst the family grieved. Then, one morning, James, the youngest of the Tillinghast boys, came down to breakfast looking pale, shivering, and complaining of a weight on his chest during the previous night. He had dreamed that Sarah had come into his room and had sat on his bed. The boy's story alarmed his mother a little, but she ascribed it to the grief that James was undoubtedly experiencing. Yet, later on in the day, the child complained of a pain just above his heart where he said that his nightmare vision of Sarah had touched him. And the following day he was even paler and his breath made an unhealthy rattling sound. Honour put him to bed and prepared some nourishing broths for him. All in vain, for shortly after, James was dead.

And now, the ghastly illness really took hold. Two more of Snuffy's children—14-year-old Andris and her sister Ruth—complained of feeling ill and debilitated and went to bed. They, too, had dreamed of Sarah and had complained of a weight on their chests as they slept. These portents were ominous, for they suggested that Sarah was returning from the dead to draw the life from the remaining members of her family. A new word began to circulate through South County: *vampire*! Snuffy began to suspect that his own nightmares had foretold the evil that had come amongst them all, and so he visited the Reverend Northup once more. Perplexed and frightened, as Snuffy was himself, the pastor reassured the terrified apple farmer that this was the Divine will and that things would right themselves in God's time. He must continue to pray.

Nevertheless, a creepy dread began to steal through Snuffy's family and across the local community where one or two others were also dying. They, too, it was rumored, had dreamed of Sarah. The notion of vampirism was gaining hold in South County.

Things came to a head when the Tillinghast's eldest daughter, Hannah (who was 26, married, and living in West Greenwich, and who had come over each day to help her mother with the invalids), began to complain of an illness. She also stated that each evening, as she left the farm to journey home, she was sure that something followed her. She slid into a kind of sick lethargy, and by the late spring of 1798, she too was dead.

Now Honour herself, who had been a mainstay of the family, began to complain of strange dreams. She dreamed that Sarah called to her from the farmyard below her bedroom window, begging her to come down and warm her. "Mama! I'm so cold!" the spectral voice called to her. Honour was already starting to feel ill as the youngest Tillinghast boy, Ezra, collapsed with the mysterious illness and was taken to bed. Snuffy knew that he had to act if he was to save his family from being wiped out. There was surmounting pressure being put on him by the community to do something about the situation. Taking Caleb, one of his strongest farmhands, he drove out early in the morning to the cemetery where Sarah had been laid to rest. He took a long-bladed hunting knife and a large container of lamp oil with him.

When they reached the spot, Snuffy made straight for his daughter's grave. He carried a shovel and a pick, and once he had reached her burial place, set to with a grim determination, unearthing her casket. It was still intact, although a little worn from having been in the earth for 18 months.

"Give me a hand," he commanded Caleb, motioning to the box. Terrified, the boy helped him fix ropes to it and haul it up beside the grave. Then he helped his master to force the lid open. It came off with a crack, and Stukley Tillinghast looked down on the body of his daughter. According to tradition, she lay there as if she were simply asleep, completely uncorrupted. Indeed, says, the legend, her still face was highly flushed as if with blood. "The oil!"

Snuffy commanded his trembling companion. "Fetch me the oil from the cart!" The boy rushed to do his bidding. Whilst he was momentarily gone, Tillinghast took his knife and cut out his daughter's heart. Blood gushed out, it is said, as though the corpse had been gorged with it. The boy returned with the lamp oil and, setting the heart on the ground beside the coffin, Snuffy set fire to it. The heart flared up like a candle, releasing clouds of dark smoke. The tiny churchyard seemed to resound with a sigh, although maybe it was only a sudden early morning breeze. The heart burned away to ash as Snuffy turned away.

His actions seemed to have the desired effect. It was too late to save young Ezra, but Honour made a full recovery. The dreams of Sarah, both in the family and in the community, ceased. But, as Stukely himself was to realize later, his original dream had in a way come true. He had dreamed that half his orchard had been decimated, and now half his family had died. Were they the victims of vampires?

Sarah Tillinghast might have been at peace, but the alleged vampire activity in rural Rhode Island was just getting underway. For a while things were quiet, but the strange malady kept bubbling under the surface to reemerge again in 1827.

Nancy Young

Nancy Young was the eldest daughter of Captain Levi Young, a military man from the remote area of Foster. Young was not a native Rhode Islander, but came from Sterling, Connecticut. However, shortly after leaving the Army, he married his sweetheart, Anna Perkins, and purchased a plot of land in the heavily wooded Foster district, settling there around 1807. Shortly thereafter, he became a reasonably prosperous farmer with a growing family that would eventually amount to eight children. By the time Nancy turned 20, she was a sharp and astute girl, well able to run and farm and do most of the ledger work for her father. The farm in Foster was a relatively happy place until...

One evening in 1827, Levi Young returned home from a trip to find his daughter suffering from what he thought was a severe cold. She went to bed and the fever appeared to grow worse. It became so bad that she could not resume her normal duties for months. These were given to her sister Almira, who struggled with them until, they hoped, Nancy got better. However, far from recovering, Nancy's condition seemed to worsen and she was now in the grip of what looked like a raging fever. On the April 6, 1827, she died and the doctor diagnosed it as galloping consumption.

Events in the Young household began to follow those that had occurred at the Tillinghast farm almost 30 years earlier. Shortly after Nancy's death, Almira also became ill with a similar condition, wasting away seemingly night after night. She told her parents that each night she dreamed of Nancy coming to visit her. Levi Young was worried, not only about his daughter's condition, but about the peculiar nightmares. Whether he knew of the Tillinghast case (and perhaps he did), he was now convinced that some sort of supernatural agency was at work and he therefore called a meeting of the community leaders to see if they could deal with the illness on a spiritual basis.

The elders decided that Levi's house was being tormented by some sort of demon, probably from the forests round about. They were persuaded to consult with a local "witch man," the so-called "Doc" Lennox (although he wasn't really a doctor). He was a white-bearded "conjurer" who treated the afflicted of the community with herbs and potions of his own concoction. He also knew about ghosts and demons. He agreed with

the elders that Nancy was possessed by some sort of dark spirit that was drawing the life from those family members around her, and would eventually go on to attack the local community. There was only one way to dismiss such spirits, he declared, and he instructed a number of local youths to gather dry brushwood in the forest and take it to the cemetery where Nancy Young lay buried.

"We're goin' t'build one Hell of a bonfire," he told the elders. Soon a large pile of wood, brought from the forest and from surrounding farms, was piled up beside the small plot where Nancy Young lay. The "Doc" then motioned that the coffin should be dug up and placed on top of the pyre. This was done, and the brushwood was then lit. Flames roared up into the evening sky, filling the tiny churchyard with a ruddy light. "Doc" Lennox advised members of the Young family to stand as close to the fire as they could so that the smoke would "wash away" the vampiric infection. They stood stock still as the vapors from the fire wafted over them. This, "Doc" Lennox assured them, would drive away the evil. It did no good, however. Less than a year afterward, Almira died with the same mysterious wasting illness, and across a space of three to four years thereafter, several more of Levi Young's family were taken by sickness. However, none of the other children were ever exhumed. Once again, the Rhode Island "vampire sickness" seemed to have passed—but only for a while. It lay like a poison in the soil, waiting.

Juliet Rose

In 1874, 53-year-old William G. Rose had more or less became a pillar of the South County community. A hard and resilient man, he had a reputation for toughness throughout his harsh life. However, he lost his daughter Juliet to a mysterious fever. Juliet had been the child of his first wife, Mary Taylor,

who had died some eight years earlier. William had been particularly fond of Juliet. In fact, he was nearly beside himself
with grief, questioning why *his* daughter should have been
stricken (the local doctor had diagnosed it as consumption,
which seems to have been a catchall illness) and, well aware
of the Tillinghast and Young cases, his thoughts turned toward the restless dead and to vampires. When, several months
after Juliet's death, his 7-year-old daughter Rosalind began to
show signs of the same mysterious fever, William became convinced that his home was under supernatural attack.

He set out to see the local priest, Father Amos Cabot, a me-
ticulous man well versed in Church doctrine. Cabot was well
aware of Juliet's recent death and of some of the things that
had been whispered about it, but, all the same, Rose's sudden
appearance unnerved him. He was even more unsettled when
he heard the wild talk about demons and vampires. He advised William to pray for the recovery of his daughter. Ignor-
ing the clergyman, William Rose stormed out—he had another
avenue that he could try.

Rose's second wife, Mary Griswold, had been married before to a Thomas Tillinghast, who had died long before she
had married William and who is thought to have been a direct
descendant of Stukley Tillinghast. Her former husband's family were well acquainted with vampires, and it was to her that
William now turned. It is doubtful as to whether Mary had told
him the full story that she'd learned of the Tillinghast family
before, but now sitting in their remote farmhouse she revealed
the horror in some detail. Mixed in with her story were some
old bits of lore that she'd picked up herself. A vampire, she said,
could live within the grave of its last victim. If he was to "liber-
ate" Juliet from the clutches of the fiend, he would have to
violate her grave by exhuming her body and destroying it. It
was the only way that he could protect his living family.

The next day, late in the evening, William Rose made his
way to the nearby cemetery where his daughter lay. As the

sun began to set he hesitated, sitting down in the gateway to contemplate the blasphemy that he was about to commit. Could he go through with it? As he sat there in the evening mist, a figure seemed to drift through the haze toward him. Looking up, he saw that it was his dead daughter Juliet.

"Papa!" she whispered, "It's so cold. I can't get any warmth." In that moment, he would have rushed to embrace her but he remembered his wife's tale and reeled back in horror. He was suddenly alone at the cemetery gate. Now convinced that something supernatural was afoot, he made his way to his daughter's grave. From underneath his coat, he produced a shovel and, without further hesitation, began to dig. After a few minutes, the blade of the shovel struck wood.

Surprisingly, the casket showed few signs of decay. With a trembling hand, William Rose lifted the lid. Juliet lay just as he had remembered her, wrapped in a winding sheet. There was little unusual about the corpse—except for the blood. It was spread across the sheet in a huge, partly dried stain. And he noticed Juliet seemed to have a high color about her, as if she'd recently ingested some blood. It was as he'd suspected and as his wife had hinted: Juliet was a vampire! Taking his knife from a little satchel that he carried, Rose bent over the open coffin and carefully cut the heart from his daughter. From beneath the shroud came a sound like a sigh, the corpse seemed to jerk and then was still once more. William reburied the coffin, and then weeping, silently left the graveyard. When he arrived home, he went straight to his room and stoked up the fire. As the flames leapt higher, Rose took a small package from his pocket and dropped it into the blaze—Juliet's heart. With an anguished cry he fell back again as smoke soared up the chimney, carrying the vampire curse away. But only for a few years.

Mercy Brown

The best-reported vampire lady is probably Mercy Brown. When Bram Stoker, author of *Dracula*, died, his wife found cuttings from some American newspapers (Stoker had been on tour in America with the actor Sir Henry Irving) all concerning the Brown case tucked away in one of his cases. It is thought to have partly influenced the writer and added an American element to the novel.

The onset of a harsh winter in 1883 marked the beginning of a dark and terrifying time for George Brown and his family. The settlement of Exeter, where they lived, was hit by a series of colds and flus that drove many of their neighbors to their beds. And a fever laid his wife, Mary, normally a healthy woman, low. As the dark days of 1883 drew in, the sickness grew worse,

and on December 8, Mary closed her eyes for the last time. The family was distraught, but worse was to follow.

As the spring of 1884 rolled round, George's eldest daughter, Mary Olive, began to show traces of the same fatal disease. She complained of dreadful dreams and was vaguely aware of a crushing weight upon her chest as she slept. She grew pale and haggard, and, as the summer came in, she began to fade more quickly. On June 6, 1884, she too passed away. Although his own grief was almost immeasurable, George Brown was a stolid working man and he desperately tried to pull his shattered family together once more. For several years, the family experienced a period of relative peace. During this time, Edwin, the Brown's only son, married and acquired a farm in nearby Wickford, where he settled with his bride, leaving his sisters to look after his father. All seemed well with the family, but the sinister shadow of vampirism was not all that far away.

Five years after the death of Mary Olive, in 1889, Edwin himself began to show signs of the same terrible disease. He too dreamed of being suffocated and began to exhibit a disturbing pallor. Local doctors professed themselves baffled by the illness. Edwin grew steadily worse, complaining that he felt as if all the blood were being drained from his body. He passed from a robust young man into a gaunt and shambling figure, moving listlessly about his yard and taking an interest in nothing. Doctors advised a change of air and suggested that he go to Colorado Springs, in the hope that his health would improve. But although Edwin set off for his cure, the shadow that blighted his family refused to go away.

In January 1892, the strange disease struck again. Still in Colorado Springs, Edwin received word that his younger sister, Mercy Lena, had taken to her bed with the same symptoms. He immediately rushed back to Rhode Island, but he was too late; by the time he arrived, his sister was already dead.

The shock drained the still-frail Edwin, and he had to stay with his father-in-law, Willis Himes, to regain at least some of his strength. The dreadful dreams of a presence in the bedroom and a crushing weight on his chest, which had all but disappeared during his time in Colorado Springs, now returned with a vengeance. Himes, concerned with his well-being, advised him to stay under his roof for as long as was necessary. Whilst there, he received a number of visitors—elders from the Exeter and Wickford communities. As they sat talking, old tales began to resurface—the stories of Juliet Rose and Nancy Young and the horror of Sarah Tillinghast. An ancient evil was loose in the area, they suggested, an evil that had to be tackled. At first Edwin Brown rejected such beliefs as mere superstition, but later he began to wonder. There seemed to be *something* lurking in the woods and forests of Rhode Island, which from time to time ventured out into the settlements round about, drinking blood and turning its victims into demons. And the more he thought about it, the more the idea took hold. At night as he slept, he saw his sister's face leaning over him, her lips red and her eyes burning.

"Edwin!" her voice pleaded, echoing through the nightmare. "I'm cold and hungry. Feed me! Please!" And he always awoke in a sweat with the bedclothes damp around him. He couldn't rest—he had to do something about this.

Because she had died during the winter when the ground was still hard and frozen, Mercy had not been buried in Exeter's tiny Chestnut Hill cemetery, but had been left—still coffined and on a cart—in a small stone crypt on the graveyard's edge. The body was still accessible. Bearing in mind some of the old stories, Edwin contacted a local doctor named Harold Metcalf who had a background in surgery. Metcalf himself was not untouched by the weird superstitions of the South County people, and was convinced that there was something uncanny about Edwin's

illness. He suggested an exhumation of Edwin's mother and elder sister, Mary Olive. With Edwin's consent this was done and the bodies were examined. Nothing was found. The moldering skeletons of Mary Brown were so decomposed that no opinion about them could be formed. Metcalf then turned his attention of Mercy, then dead for some nine weeks, whose body still lay within the tiny crypt.

At 5:30 on the morning of March 18, 1892, a small group of men, with Metcalf at its head and the gaunt form of Edwin Brown following, made its way to the narrow building. Many were carrying torches and some were praying. The old sexton opened the door and the men stepped inside—into the dark.

Mercy's coffin still lay on the cart and the flickering torches of the men cast eerie shadows across it. Metcalf was still very wary about the whole enterprise—he was superstitious but he was also a practical man in many respects. What if he was wrong? With a shaking voice he instructed the old caretaker to lift the coffin lid.

The men drew back; praying more earnestly now as the old man drew a pair of pliers from his pocket and started to ease the nails from the casket. There was a shriek that echoed around the tomb as each one came free but, at last, the lid was ready to lift. Metcalf and some of the other elders looked down on the corpse of Mercy Brown. After nine weeks there should have been some visible trace pf decomposition, but there was none. Mercy lay as if she were asleep, her skin slightly ruddy in the torchlight, and around the edges of her mouth were the faintest traces of blood. Taking out a small scalpel from the black doctor's bag that he carried, Metcalf leaned even further forward until he was directly above her breast. Then, almost like a frenzied ghoul, he began to cut into the flesh, creating a cavity into which he reached to pull out her heart. Reaching back in again, he extended the cut and took out her liver as well. A fine mist of blood fell from the organs settling on the floor. Although it was probably no more than would have been extracted from another cadaver, it was taken as evidence that Mercy was a supernatural creature, which had gorged itself with blood. A sound like a sigh passed through the crypt, but it may have been no more than the morning wind in the cemetery outside.

Leaving the building, Metcalf carried the organs to a corner of the burying ground where they were doused with oil and vinegar. Lifting a taper that he'd lit from a torch, Edwin Brown burned the remains of his dead sister. A boiling water and vinegar mixture was poured into the still-open coffin, over the remains that lay there. It was hoped that this marked the end of whatever had beset the Brown family and the Exeter community.

Word of these rather exotic events leaked out to a wider American public almost immediately. The leading newspaper, the *Providence Journal*, for March 19, 1892, ran with sensationalist headlines "EXHUMED THE BODIES. Testing A Horrible Superstition in the Town of Exeter. BODIES OF DEAD RELATIVES TAKEN FROM THEIR GRAVES." Two days later, the same newspaper was to proclaim "VAMPIRE THEORY: THAT SEARCH FOR THE SPECTRAL GHOUL IN THE EXETER GRAVES." Old alleged vampire cases in the area and in surrounding states were swiftly revived— Horace Ray in Jewett City, Connecticut (1854); a family named Corwen in Woodstock, Vermont (reported in the *Vermont Standard* in 1834); and a peculiar case in Manchester, Vermont. All these pointed to a New England vampire tradition that fascinated much of America.

The macabre events in Chestnut Hill Cemetery in the winter of 1892 proved too much for the frail Edwin Brown. Within several months, he was dead, and with his death the vampire curse seemed to have finally lifted from Rhode Island.

Nevertheless, it seems to have left a legacy behind—a legacy of mystery and speculation, which may have partly inspired Bram Stoker to write his famous novel.

That leaves only Nelly Vaughan in her grave in Coventry, South County. Nothing is known about her or her life, but the mysterious inscription on her tombstone was to provoke wonder and apprehension.

"I am waiting and watching for you."

What did it mean? Maybe there was a simple explanation—a message to a beloved family or some special sweetheart—but we shall never know. Some, however, have suggested that there is a much more sinister meaning to the message. The inscription came to a wider American audience when *Yankee* magazine published an article titled "The Words on Nelly's Tombstone," which provoked a great deal of interest, especially from occultists but also from the religiously inclined. Indeed, the tombstone had to be removed in the early 1990s to prevent it from being desecrated by religious fundamentalists and vampire hunters. One astute individual has pointed out that many of the homes of the so-called "Vampire Ladies" lie along Route 102, which has subsequently been named "Rhode Island's Vampire Highway."

Of course, the events surrounding the Vampire Ladies of Rhode Island can be logically interpreted. A recurrent epidemic of tuberculosis coupled with a credulous, almost hysterical turn of mind is a common answer, and the newspapers of the time (and subsequent publications) have sought to portray these early Rhode Islanders as gullible, superstitious people. But, though we may scoff at such "primitive beliefs"

there just might be a hint of wariness in our tone. Maybe there *is* something lurking out there in the dark New England woods—something that is waiting and watching!

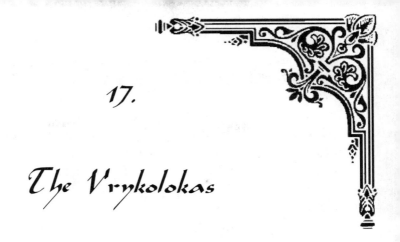

17.

The Vrykolokas

GREECE

As with many other cultures, the vampirology of Greece is often both complex and confusing. The great cultural antiquity adds to such complexity, for the origin of the vampire belief lies far back in time. Indeed, the first idea of distinct Greek vampires seems to have developed around 586–587 C.E., after an immigration of both Turkish and Slavic peasants into the northern part of the region. This, however, is not to say that there were not vampiric entities in Greek folklore before this time.

The Lamia

One of the earliest malignant and life-threatening supernatural forms that displayed vampire characteristics was that of a *lamia*, usually a female or hermaphroditic demon that

prowled among human settlements after dark. This monster's prey was usually sleeping infants whom she stole from their cradles and removed to her lair, where she drank their blood. The lamia is described as having the head and breasts of a woman, but the lower body of a serpent.

According to Greek legend, Lamia was once a beautiful Libyan princess, the daughter of Belus and Libya, with whom the god Zeus fell in love and seduced. The goddess Hera, wife of Zeus, grew jealous of the union and, in a fit of fury, killed all of Lamia's children, who had been fathered by the god, driving the unfortunate princess into a cave in the remote desert. Hera transformed her into a hideous, ravening monster.

Like many other vampires, the lsamia could also allegedly alter her appearance into a more pleasing form. For example, from time to time, she took on the appearance of a pretty young woman in order to lure men into her clutches, so she could kill them. An ancient legend recorded in the *Life of Appolonus* tells of how a pupil named Menippus, of the first-century philosopher and magician Apollonius of Tyana, became attracted to a rich and beautiful noblewoman and proposed marriage to her. Apollonius himself, however, was able to see beyond the disguise and warned the youth that his fiancé was in reality a blood-drinking lamia. Menippus was not to be turned, and so the sage confronted the monster, forcing her to reveal her true form.

In some respects, the lamia resembled the early Sumerian demon-goddess Lilith, who also appears in Hebrew mythology as Adam's first wife. Both of these entities spawned hundreds of demons that both attacked and killed individuals. These demons were known to the ancient Greeks as *empusa* (vampires) or *mormolykiai* (hobgoblins), and were incredibly hostile toward mankind. There were also returning revenants—humans who had died and had come back in a tangible, physical form—in the ancient Greek world, though whether or not they drank blood is unclear. Like the lamia, their victims were usually small children or the old, weak, and infirm. In some versions, the empusa attended upon the goddess Hecate, ruler of night and the underworld. Another type of night-visitor—the *mormo* or "bogeyman" whose specific victims were unruly or disobedient children—may also have had vampiric qualities, as did the *gelloudes* and *stringla*, female demons who lurked in the shadows and crept up on the cribs of sleeping infants to draw small quantities of blood from them. This belief was often used to explain a child's failure to thrive or why it was sickly and irritable. These demons also sometimes attacked young, sleeping men, draining them of semen and taking away their virility as well as their strength.

The Returning Dead

Gradually, the notion of demons as wholly supernatural beings began to decline and the idea of revenants—the returning dead—took over. This may have been due to a concern over the proper performance of funerary rites. J.C. Lawson, in his *Modern Greek Folklore and Ancient Greek Religion* (1910), along with several other authorities, cites a well-known story of the nightly return of Philinnion, a recently deceased young woman, for sexual liaisons with a guest in her grieving parents' house. There is no suggestion that the girl was a ravening demon in the style of the lamia; she simply is depicted as a corpse that would not lie still in its grave. Why this is so is not clear, but there is a suggestion that it might be because the girl was not buried properly—that is, the proper rites were not observed. Alternatively, Lawson suggests that there may be some element of vengeance in her return (the girl may have been murdered) and he uses retribution as an explanation for the return of the Greek dead. The reasons for such a return were indeed rather complex. It is, however, interesting to note that the girl's nightly visits only stopped when her body had

been removed from the grave and cremated. In fact, cremation would become an essential feature in dealing with Greek vampires.

Emergence of the Vrykolokas

From roughly around the 17th century, when Christianity had taken a firm hold in Greece, the two ideas—the notion of demons and the belief in the returning dead—began to combine and intermingle. It was now believed that revenants were the physical and corporeal bodies of the recently dead, which were animated by some awful demon. Such corpses were known by a number of names depending upon the region of Greece in which they appeared. On Crete, for example, they were known as *kathakanas*, whereas on the Greek archipelago they were known as *vurvukalas*, or *vrukokalas*. On the Adriatic and Aegean coastlines, however, they were termed *vrykolokas* and this became a generally accepted description in other parts of Greece as well. The name always referred to the returning dead who would perhaps drink blood or do mortals some sort of harm.

The ways in which a corpse could become a vampire were many and varied. The Greek Undead consisted of:

- Those who were stillborn or who had otherwise died without receiving the rites of the Church or benefit of clergy.
- Those who were conceived or born on a Holy Day, which was considered to be a great blasphemy.
- Those who ate the flesh of an animal that had been accidentally killed and not properly slaughtered.
- Those who had not received a proper religious burial with the proper funerary rites and rituals.
- Those who were of Turkish extraction. This referred to ancient animosities that had existed between some Greeks and the Turks.

- ❧ Those who died having led sinful lives.
- ❧ Those who died under excommunication by the Church or who were considered apostates.
- ❧ Those who had practiced sorcery or witchcraft whilst alive.
- ❧ Those who had committed a sexual act with an animal. It was widely believed that this particular sin would invariably result in an individual becoming a vampire, even though the sinner might have been granted absolution.
- ❧ Those whose corpse had been passed over by an animal before burial. Measures were often taken to prevent dogs and cats from jumping over the body whilst it lay in public view.
- ❧ Those who had died from a plague or unknown disease. The thinking behind this was that it was believed that vampires actually *spread* disease and so it was likely that the deceased had already been in some sort of contact with vrykolokas.
- ❧ Those who had been prostitutes, both male and female, or who had committed a sexual act with a foreigner. Once again, a certain xenophobia lies at the heart of such a belief.
- ❧ Those who had been cursed by a priest or holy man.
- ❧ Those who had been scolds or unpleasant people in life.

There were also other minor reasons as to why a person could become a vampire. To further confuse matters, even if someone met any of these criteria, it did not necessarily mean that he or she would become blood-drinkers. It might simply mean that he or she could not rest easy in his or her grave and would take to wandering about as a sort of corporeal ghost. These were originally known as *alastores* or "Wanderers"— spirits trapped in a kind of limbo, wandering ceaselessly and

without rest. An ancient Greek curse—"May the ground not receive thee" or "May death reject thee"—seems to sum up their position. Occasionally, however, the corpses took advantage of their situation to settle old scores with their enemies or with people whom they had disliked in life. Because such vengeance was often associated with blood or death, some commentators have invoked the notion of a "blood-feud" similar to those that existed in parts of Italy. This led to the idea of a vengeful class of revenants, *miastores* and *prostropaioi*, whilst harmless "Wanderers" now became nameless.

It may be that some of these wandering souls may have drunk blood; indeed, it was believed in some parts of Greece that some revenants did not have the power to speak until they had tasted blood—though not necessarily human blood. The origins of this belief may lie in the ancient tale of Odysseus, as recounted in the *Iliad*. In order to commune with the spirit of the seer Tirsias, Odysseus has to fill a pit with sheep's blood so that the ghost can drink. After that, Tirsias can speak and tell Odysseus what he wishes to know. Other ghosts also come to the pit to drink and can then converse with him, but, as he speaks to the shade of his mother, he attempts to embrace her and she vanishes. Blood was important to the wandering dead, for it served as food.

Nor were any of the Greek vampires confined to the hours of darkness. For many ancient peoples, the stroke of midday (the crossing over between morning and afternoon/evening) was just as fraught with supernatural danger as was midnight. The dead—wanderers and more dangerous ghosts—might be found moving about in the daylight just as they might be at night. On the surface, they might be indistinguishable from any mortal, although there were certain telltale signs: they had a lost and vacant stare about them; they cast no shadow; they did not eat; and their hair had a faint reddish tinge to it. Such people should be strenuously avoided, said local Greek wisdom.

Traits of the Vrykolokas

Most dangerous of all the wanderers were the vrykolokas. The word, say some sources, is not Greek at all, but Slavic, meaning "wolf." Although, according to Leone Allacci (*De quorundam Graecorum Opinationibus* "*On certain modern opinions among the Greeks,*" 1645), the word is taken from older sources and means "cesspool," "midden," or "filthy place." Those who were believed to have been werewolves would have performed a sexual act with an animal or had been cursed by a bishop (not a priest) would become this dangerous form of vampire. However, the Greeks did not use the word *vampire* to describe the revenant, although the word *vampiras* does appear in some areas, but it is used as a term of contempt or abuse toward a living person.

It is commonly agreed that vrykolokas are animated directly by the Devil or by some evil spirit. Their purpose is to lure God-fearing people away from the paths of righteousness and into wickedness and death. In some parts of Greece—for example, on the island of Chios—people will not answer to their names being called until the caller has repeated it for a second time, in case it is one of the vrykolokas who is calling them. The belief is that if the cry is answered, the victim will die within 24 hours.

Because it is almost a form of devil, it is believed that the vampire can alter its shape to appear alluring or handsome. Daylight, however, often forces it to resume its true form for brief periods of time—a form that is so ugly that all who see it die from fright. If, however, an individual invokes the name of God or the name of an angel, then the thing disappears immediately.

From time to time, vrykolokas might be spotted in the fields, usually around midday, eating corn or beans and troubling no one. Some might even enter houses, when the owners were out and always in daylight, and help themselves to a few scraps of food that were lying around, without actually

disturbing anybody. Their presence, however, was enough to alarm local communities that often immediately requested that nearby graves be examined.

Sometimes the vrykolokas can be maliciously playful, pulling the bedclothes of sleeping people, eating food or drinking wine that has been left out for the next day's meal, mocking people on their way to church, waking up the priest as if for matins when it is not time, and throwing stones at travellers in a particular road. They might also break jugs, spill liquids on the floor, or simply be generally abusive both to people and property. Exorcism and prayer will often drive them away,

The Tympaniaosis

A type of vampire known as *tympaniaois*, meaning "like a drum," swells up like a balloon, possibly from the blood that it has ingested, whilst in its tomb. These vampires are reputedly sluggish and torpid, and venture out only occasionally and then during daylight hours. The destruction of these creatures can only be accomplished on a Saturday—the ancient Hebrew holy day of rest, when all of these creatures are said to sleep in the grave. It is also thought that vrykolokas have distended limbs with which they can sometimes grab those who have come to destroy them or those who venture too close to their tombs. They must, therefore, be approached with caution.

Destroying a Vrykolokas

In some parts of Greece it is believed that the only person who can effectively destroy the vrykolokas is a bishop, because it is Satan who controls the Undead, and local priests are impotent against the wiles of the evil one. When a village is beset by the attentions of the vrykolokas, says one text (*Relation de l'Isle de Saint-erini*, 1657), the inhabitants must apply to the bishop to have a suspected tomb opened. If the body is swollen or bloated (*tympanaois*) or is gorged with fresh blood, then it is adjudged to be one of the vrykolokas and the bishop is called upon to perform an exorcism. Most of these tombs are opened on Saturdays and the exorcism performed that day. In former days, the ritual consisted mainly of prayer and, if these were effective, then the body dissolved away before the eyes of the villagers. If the exorcism failed and prayer was ineffective, the body was ritually cremated and the ashes scattered.

The thronging Greek dead, therefore, offer a highly complex cultural tapestry. General wandering spirits, fragmentary legends concerning old gods, Christian demonology, and local stories concerning returning revenants have all added to the confusion. And yet, beyond all this complexity, there is one certain truth: the malignant dead are not far away, at any time. They are watching and waiting with intentions of their own, ready to enter the world of the living. We should truly be very afraid.

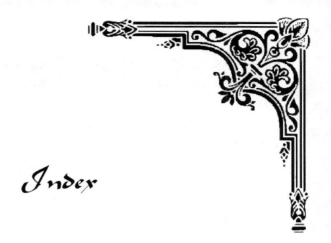

Index

About the Author and Illustrator

Dr. Bob Curran was born in a rural area of County Down, Northern Ireland. On leaving school he worked at many jobs, including journalism, music, truck driving, and grave digging. He travelled in America, North Africa, and Holland before returning to Northern Ireland to settle down and obtain degrees in history and education and a doctorate in educational pscyhology. From his early years, he has been interested in folktales and legends and has made a study of these, writing widely in books and magazines. His work has been printed in his native Ireland, Great Britain, France, Germany, and Japan. Still lecturing and teaching, he lives in County Derry with his wife and young family.

Ian Daniels works professionally as a painter and illustrator. His work includes themes of earth and spirit, nature, dreaming, memory, ghosts, and ancient mythology. His previous

illustration projects range from children's fairytales to fantasy fiction and gothic romance, including book covers for Edgar Allen Poe, Marion Zimmer Bradley, Orson Scott Card, and Poul Anderson. He has also illustrated two collections of fairytales, *Classic Celtic Fairytales* and *Tales of the Celtic Otherworld*, which feature many of his visionary paintings. Ian lives in Kent, England.